NORTH CHICAGO
PUBLIC LIBRARY

PENGUIN BOO

STOPPING AT E'

LEMONADE STA

James Vollbracht is an international trainer, speaker, and author with more than twenty years of experience empowering individuals, communities, and organizations in the positive development of youth. As president of Higher Ground Associates, Vollbracht has been the keynote speaker at numerous national conferences, and a recent presentation was carried live over CFAX Radio, in Victoria, B.C., to an audience of over 20,000. In August of 2000, Vollbracht was honored as Delta's Flyer of the Month for his work in building strong, healthy, and connected communities for youth across North America. He has written three children's books that draw upon the rich spiritual traditions of the world, and that are designed to teach universal values and character. He lives in Bozeman, Montana, and is the father of four great kids.

Stopping at Every

Lemonade Stand

HOW TO CREATE A CULTURE
THAT CARES FOR KIDS

JAMES R. VOLLBRACHT

NORTH CHICAGO
PUBLIC LIBRARY

305.23
VOL

Penguin Books

PENGUIN BOOKS

Published by the Penguin Group

Penguin Putnam Inc., 375 Hudson Street,
New York, New York 10014, U.S.A.
Penguin Books Ltd, 27 Wrights Lane,
London W8 5TZ, England
Penguin Books Australia Ltd, Ringwood,
Victoria, Australia
Penguin Books Canada Ltd, 10 Alcorn Avenue,
Toronto, Ontario, Canada M4V 3B2
Penguin Books (N.Z.) Ltd, 182-190 Wairau Road,
Auckland 10, New Zealand

Penguin Books Ltd, Registered Offices:
Harmondsworth, Middlesex, England

First published in Penguin Books 2001

1 3 5 7 9 10 8 6 4 2

Copyright © James Vollbracht, 2001

All rights reserved

LIBRARY OF CONGRESS CATALOGING IN PUBLICATION DATA
Vollbracht, James R., 1950–
Stopping at every lemonade stand : how to create a culture
that cares for kids / James R. Vollbracht.
p.   cm.
ISBN 0-14-100150-x (pbk.)
1. Children—United States—Social conditions.
2. Child welfare—United States.   3. Community life—United States.
4. Children and adults—United States.   I. Title.

HQ792.U5 V65 2001
305.23'0973—dc21   00-065230

Printed in the United States of America
Set in Adobe Minion
Designed by Johanna Roebas

Except in the United States of America, this book is sold subject
to the condition that it shall not, by way of trade or otherwise, be lent,
re-sold, hired out, or otherwise circulated without the publisher's prior
consent in any form of binding or cover other than that in which it is
published and without a similar condition including this condition being
imposed on the subsequent purchaser.

To my family

Acknowledgments

I'd like to acknowledge all the wonderful people who have shared their heartwarming stories of how to create a more connected community of kids, Rich Little, Joyce Phelps, and the fabulous folks at Quest International for teaching me so much, Alice Levine, Peter Benson and Search Institute for their great work with kids, and to my own family who provided me with lots of material for the book.

If you'd like to share your own inspirational story about how ordinary kids and adults are doing extraordinary things to create a culture that cares about kids, or if you'd like to learn more about keynote presentations and workshops by James Vollbracht, visit his website
<www. lemonade-stand.com>

Contents

ix

Introduction

As I was driving through my neighborhood on a hot summer day, I saw something I had not seen in a very long time: a lemonade stand. Jumping up and down around a small folding table were four of the neighborhood's children, waving their hand-made signs and desperately trying to make contact with each car that passed by. As I slowed down, their faces brightened, and before I could even open my car door, several children were huddled outside my window clamoring excitedly, "Would you like to buy some lemonade, mister? Only twenty-five cents!"

If there is such a thing as a contact high, I caught it. Rolling down my window, I gazed into their shiny faces and asked, "How long have you been in business?" "All morning," they sang out in one enthusiastic chorus. I glanced over at the table. Something about it looked strangely familiar—almost timeless. A stained white tablecloth flapped a bit in the wind. There was an old plastic pitcher brimming with ice cubes and dripping in the heat of the afternoon sun. A shoebox that I guessed must have been the bank sat open and exposed. For a moment I felt as if I were ten years old again. The enterprise looked identical to the one that Charlie Monary and I used to run in our old neighborhood. We did one thing and we did it very well: we sold cherry Kool-Aid with lots of ice cubes. We figured that because Kool-Aid cost only five cents a pack, we could make a bundle. To be sure we didn't miss the bike trade, we even had a place set aside for kids to park their "wheels."

As I got out of my car, I walked slowly toward the lemonade stand, savoring the simplicity of the moment. I had one choice: lemonade. I realized that regardless of what these kids were selling, I was buying. "I'll take four cups," I said, getting a little carried away. Their faces lit up and they rushed to fill my order. One poured. One wiped up a small spill. One jiggled the change box. Another pulled out a plastic bucket full of ice cubes that was hidden under the table. I watched, intrigued, as a dirty hand plopped ice cubes of assorted sizes into my four cups! "Hmm," I mused, "organic lemonade."

Amidst this flurry of activity, a jogger approached the stand. "Want some lemonade, mister?" three of them screeched with that same incredible enthusiasm. Looking really sweaty and a little embarrassed, he replied sheepishly, "I do, but I don't have any money." As I fished around in my pocket for a quarter to cover for him, one of the girls blurted out, "That's okay, you can have it for free!" The jogger and I made eye contact and we both smiled. "What a great marketing strategy," I thought. And in that moment I realized what was so wonderful about lemonade stands: kids weren't selling, they were giving. They were giving the gifts that children innately give: excitement, optimism, sharing, connection, and profound innocence. As I reflected upon the past few moments, I realized that I had already received far more than I had given. I was having a very close encounter with the most important resource in our community: our youth!

I watched as these entrepreneurs tended to their newest customer. I noticed cars zipping by and faces staring out from behind windows trying to figure out what this scene was all about. It seemed to me the occupants truly wanted to stop, but, for whatever reason, the drivers couldn't seem to find the brakes in time. "How sad," I thought. "This is an important community event. This is where the action really is!"

After paying for my lemonade and tipping generously, I realized that I had no idea what to do with four cups of organic lemonade. "I'd like to donate three of these to any deserving customers who pass by," I told them. Thanking me, they dumped the lemonade back into the pitcher. Scooping up my single cup, I climbed into my car. As I drove away, it occurred to me that it had been years since I had seen a lemonade stand. Maybe parents are worried that their children aren't safe in the public eye. Maybe today's kids are too busy with activities, and too hypnotized by their computers. Or maybe we've all just forgotten how much fun lemonade stands are and how vital they can be to the neighborhood.

In that moment, I made a vow that might sound kind of silly, but it made a lot of sense to me. I vowed to stop at every lemonade stand I saw. And I vowed to invest as much emotionally and financially as I could in each of these. About one block later I finally sampled the product. It was so sour my entire mouth and throat immediately puckered in a huge protest and my eyes filled with tears. Pulling over to dump it out, I glanced down the street to make sure the young entrepreneurs couldn't see me. There they were, waving and hollering at cars as they zoomed by. "Hmm," I pondered, "maybe I'll circle around the block and stop again. This is the most fun I've had in a long time!"

Although the impetus for this book grew out of that delightful moment, I actually ~~had~~ begun thinking about it a long time ago, when I was twentysomething, single, going to college, and working part-time in the public schools to make ends meet. It was there my idealism met with reality. I had just stepped off a bus outside the middle school where I taught when I saw a bunch of kids gathering quickly behind the gym. The atmosphere was charged and all around me were excited shouts of "Fight!" I remember thinking, "This isn't in my job description," as I waded through the crowd. Typically in a situation like this, one of the kids would want a way out and my arrival would provide the perfect opportunity. But this time, when I got inside the circle, I froze. This was no typical fight.

It was a hair-pulling, fingernail-flashing, no-holds-barred fight between two girls. While they circled and screamed profanities at each other, the growing crowd urged them on. Another teacher showed up and the energy somehow turned on us. "Leave 'em alone," one of the onlookers shouted. A student vented, "It's none of your business!" Fortunately, at that moment, the huge gym teacher bulled his way into the circle. We managed to bring it to an end.

The three of us headed back to the school, shell-shocked. We tried to talk about it, but bells were ringing and we had to get to our classes. As I thought about the incident throughout the day, I realized it wasn't just the fight that was so bizarre. It was everything that came along with it—the language, the disregard for our authority, the onlookers' support of the violence. As I reflect upon this event some twenty years later, it seems to me there had been alarms going off everywhere. We knew something was going very wrong, but for the most part, we just didn't know what to do.

Now, raising four kids in today's culture, I feel as if I'm under siege. With one hand, I'm trying to model and teach positive values and morals to my kids, and with the other I'm trying to protect them from an assaultive culture that projects just the opposite. The fight I witnessed so long ago now seems minor compared to what kids have to deal with today. Whether it's rural, urban, or suburban America, some of our kids are now armed, dangerous, and acting out their anger in outrageous ways. We are being confronted with the realization that, wherever we live, there are no safe havens and that all kids in today's culture are at risk.

I've noticed a pattern in the reactions that follow some horrible tragedy. The media rush in and ask mayors, counselors, parents, and experts, "What went wrong?" "Did you see it coming?" "What are you going to do?" Few have any real answers but almost all share a profound sense of despair. Some point the finger at the media. Others say it's the fault of parents. And many, not knowing what else to do, start cocooning even deeper into their own worlds.

I have come to believe that our kids are not lost all at once, but rather in small steps that are directly linked to the erosion of our culture. Every time television shows push the envelope with very adult themes in prime time, every time producers in the movie industry choose to make violence entertaining, every time parents who feel so desperately alone and afraid of their surroundings pull their kids out of local schools and move to a "safer" neighborhood, and every time parents have to work long hours just to make it financially—and in so doing end up leaving their kids alone—a piece falls out of the scaffolding that holds up a healthy culture.

With so many supports missing, I sometimes wonder what is keeping us and our children from falling into an abyss.

Our culture has become a breeding ground for virtually all the behaviors we abhor, yet we are shocked when they appear in our children. What was once abnormal has become the norm. Behaviors and language that were considered outrageous just a few years ago have become a part of everyday life. We must remember that children are very new to the world and don't have the sense of context that we do. Everything they see, hear, and experience becomes a part of them. We are stewards of this most important resource, to which we have unquestionable responsibilities: to shield them from harmful and inappropriate experiences, to provide them with opportunities and invitations to participate in the life of the community that will allow their innate gifts to unfold naturally, to guide them through important rites of passage, and to love them unconditionally.

If we do not fulfill our responsibilities, the unthinkable happens. And it is happening right now. Our children, who are reflections of our culture, are being abandoned, and many are falling between the cracks. And the pace has accelerated. But this is not a book about blame. This is a book about hope, about raising happier children and creating a better future for them. It is filled with anecdotes that call us back to the bittersweet moments of our own youth and encourage us to help create new and more hopeful stories for today's children. It provides tangible steps that parents, neighbors, and community members can follow to use our influence to make a difference right now.

After teaching high school, working in alternative education environments and with special-education kids, and traveling across North America for over fifteen years as a consultant and trainer helping parents, professionals, and community members create and restore healthy community environments for our kids, I have come to realize that it's the small things that will truly have the power to transform our culture and our communities. Simple acts of the heart, when multiplied a thousand times over, become a way of life. From saying "Hi" to a kid we pass on the street, to buying lemonade no matter how it tastes, to engaging children in conversations that will make them feel valued and respected—these actions send ripples of powerful change through our communities. Having gathered stories from rural Sundance, Wyoming, to inner-city Baltimore, to the suburbs of Seattle, it's my experience that when people hear what others are doing to create positive, healthy communities for our kids, their immediate response is "I can do that!" and it is then and there that the exciting process of restoring a kid-friendly culture begins.

So exactly where do we start? Just as the culture can slip away in increments, so can we rebuild it one piece at a time. So we start small, in our own walk through life—in our families and neighborhoods, in our faith communities and the business world. By linking up our youth with the incredible untapped resource of our elders. As we expand our actions and influence one little step at a time, we will be contributing to a quiet revolution that will restore the type of culture that is healthy for our kids, and, hence, healthy for us all. It can all begin by stopping at every lemonade stand. Who knows? For a quarter and a smile, you might begin to save the world.

ONE

Our Children and the Six Circles of Community

*It is threads, hundreds of tiny threads,
which sew people together through the years.*
—SIMONE SIGNORET

When I was growing up in Seattle, after our family dinner I'd head outside, play until dark, and not go home until Dad stood out on the front porch and whistled or hollered for me to come in. On weekends my friends and I would revel in massive football or baseball games. Or if it was Seafair season, in late summer when the high hydroplane roared across Lake Washington, we would tie homemade hydroplanes to the backs of our bikes and race up and down the street. I remember big Sunday dinners with grandmas, aunts, and uncles in attendance and all of us consuming delicious meals of pot roast and great homemade desserts. On summer nights all the kids on the block would congregate next to the only telephone pole that had a light on it and play hide-and-seek until we dropped. My piano teacher lived only five houses away, and when I needed a haircut I walked the three blocks to Don's Barber Shop. If I needed help, I could knock on the doors of six or eight different homes and somebody would let me in.

The environment around me was like a pond into which a stone had been thrown. It contained circles within circles of support, starting at home and moving out through the neighborhood, nearby playgrounds, local businesses, and into the greater community. Within these circles were the universal forces that are the ultimate threads of our communities: the forces of love, of trust, and of caring. These threads that connected us to each other were constantly being rewoven each time we played a game on our sidewalk or street, attended monthly Cub Scout meetings (where both adults and kids showed up), or went next door to borrow something. The world was whole, the faces were familiar, and the streets were safe to roam.

In my work with community members and organizations across the country, I continually refer to six specific interconnected circles, represented by the individual, the family, the neighborhood, the community, businesses and government, and elders. Each chapter of this book will focus on one of these circles and on stories and strategies that speak of making a difference within that circle.

Throughout history, teachers and sages have spoken of the interconnectedness of all life. One of the very first to articulate this idea was Confucius, the master teacher and sage of China, who lived in 551–479 B.C. He taught his students that life was composed of a series of interconnected circles, each of which had a powerful reciprocal effect upon the other and on all of life:

When the ancients wished to illustrate virtue throughout the
  kingdom, they first ordered their own states.
Wishing to order well their states, they first regulated their families.
Wishing to regulate their families, they first cultivated their persons.
Wishing to cultivate their persons, they first changed their hearts.
Wishing to change their hearts, they first sought to be sincere in
  thought.
Wishing to be sincere in their thoughts, they first sought true
  knowledge within the soul.

More than 2,000 years later, Chief Seattle, one of the last great leaders of the native tribes in the Pacific Northwest, articulated this same philosophy: "All things are connected, like the blood which unites us all. Man did not weave the web of life; he is merely a strand in it. Whatever he does to the web, he does to himself."

Today, we would call this concept, which recognizes that ultimately everything is connected to everything else, a *systems approach*. Each time we open the door for someone, give up our seat on a bus or the subway, or respond to the beautiful face of a child, we reinforce the circles within our community life. Dr. Urie Bronfrenbrenner of Cornell University likens this systems approach to a set of Russian nesting dolls. Each of us is an integral yet distinct part of the whole.

The smallest of acts within one of the circles can reverberate across the entire web of a community and can affect the lives of all within it. Each time we share our gifts and take positive action we become more powerful and all the circles within the community are strengthened. However, in our current environment, many of the threads that connect us are frayed or broken, and there are wide gaps between the circles of our lives. When a disconnect occurs, not only do adults suffer, but our kids fall between the cracks and become casualties.

It seems to me that many people in America have decided that to create change we must act at a national level. We've proclaimed a "war" on drugs, developed comprehensive stop-the-violence programs, and have funded massive initiatives to prevent teen pregnancies. But our efforts are like those of Hercules facing Hydra, the many-headed monster. As we cut off one of the heads, two more appear. One year, marijuana use declines but inhalant use soars. Another year, HIV/AIDS cases decrease, but teen pregnancies are astronomical. The number of kids in gangs drops, but the number of shootings and incidents with handguns in schools goes off the charts. We've added the tragedy of runaways and homeless kids to the list, and just when you think you couldn't add another item, teen gambling increases and a new phenomenon such as "car surfing" emerges. (Haven't heard of "car surfing"? Kids jump onto the hood or the top of a car and attempt to maintain their balance as the car accelerates. When the driver slams on the brakes, the "surfer" gets points if he lands on his feet when he falls off. If he hits his head, he loses more than points.)

In this fast-paced "info-culture," any new local rage and high-risk behavior can quickly spread. We're such a wired and mobile culture that local events can become global ones overnight. So, rather than continually declaring war on all the problems and their various manifestations, we really need to start thinking in a different way about what we can achieve on an individual and local level. We need to think about mobilizing people, not programs.

In our attempts to deal with these challenges, most of us have utilized an approach that is really one-dimensional in nature: the problem-solving approach. But it's hard to get to the "solution" part. Let's say you attend a workshop on at-risk kids. When you enter the room, you notice the entire wall is plastered with chart paper. The facilitator (and it could have been me) poses the question, "What are all the problems or concerns that you have about our kids?" You spend the next hour brainstorming and prioritizing all the challenges you can think of that kids in your community face. In some ways the process feels good. You've been worried about these issues for a long time and when you get your chance, you unload. When you're all done, you have a great list of problems to attack over the next few months or even a year. But if you're like me, after you review the list, you're so overwhelmed by the challenges and the problems that all you want to do is go home and lie down. As a friend said, it's somewhat akin to a pilot explaining his plane crash: "I ran out of airspeed, altitude, and ideas simultaneously."

We have been operating from an outdated medical model that goes after the symptoms rather than the causes. In his book *Trends 2000*, Gerald Celente puts this approach in perspective.

> Certainly, in recorded history there has never been an emergency medical technology as effective as twentieth-century Western medicine. . . . Twentieth-century medicine also relieves symptoms often swiftly and spectacularly. But it is not really designed to cure. It treats the disease rather than the patient. In a civilization obsessed with fast food, instant gratification, and the quick fix, people routinely become prescription-drug junkies, endlessly popping pills just to keep the symptoms at bay or under control.

Like Western medicine's symptom-oriented treatment, our problem-solving approach has not really gone to the causation level of what's needed to remedy our communities. It overlooks the patient. Networks that were once taken for granted have all but disappeared across the six circles of community. Many people today live in one community, go to work in another, and attend religious services in another; their children are bussed halfway across town to go to school in yet another. Many kids live far from their extended families, come home to empty houses after school, and don't know their neighbors, much less anyone else on the block. We're probably not going to return to the days of *Leave It to Beaver* (until Ward and June start a home business), so we must be creative in restoring the connections that have been severed. One of the most powerful but dormant networks that needs to be restored immediately is that among parents. Because so many of our relationships are cross-community, it is imperative that parents make efforts to connect with each other, with their schools, and with their children's friends' parents.

Ever had a phone call like this? We have: It's one in the morning. The phone rings. "Hello," you answer in a daze. "This is the police," a voice says. "Would you please come down to the station? Your child is here. She was at a party." Your first response is, "You must be mistaken. Our daughter is spending the night at a friend's house. We checked it all out. Sorry, you must have the wrong number." But then suddenly the reality sets in. "Really?" you say, speechless and numb. Moments later, having thrown on some clothes, you are in your car headed for the station.

Monday morning you show up in youth court. What an education. The place is awash with kids who have been busted over the weekend—very young kids with very weary-looking parents. You feel out of place, thinking it's only other people's kids who end up here, and as you gaze around the courtroom the impact is more profound than all the research in the world. These kids, our kids, are at risk at a very early age. In this highly toxic culture, no child or teenager is immune, and it doesn't matter if you live in rural, urban, or suburban America. Kids, the hope and future of our culture, are being busted for drinking, using drugs, shoplifting, carrying weapons, and other assorted crimes. Twenty years ago the kids charged with such offenses were seventeen, eighteen, nineteen, and twenty. Now they're ten, eleven, twelve, and thirteen.

We stood with our thirteen-year-old daughter in front of the judge, who handed out the usual fines and mandatory community service sentences to her. And then we were free to go. As we left, I felt disconnected and powerless and as though something had been missing from the proceedings. It wasn't until the next day that I realized what. In retrospect, I wish the judge had made it mandatory for all the parents of the kids who were at our daughter's friend's party to meet, to get to know each other, to talk about what happened, and to act in concert so our kids wouldn't fall between the cracks again.

Underlying the surface of our culture and our communities are powerful organic forces waiting to be tapped. We don't live in isolation; the ability to create a healthy community for our kids is reliant upon the intent and action of everyone across the six circles. As we begin to realize this, we can start replacing despair with hope and taking personal responsibility instead of blaming others. One of the first things we need to realize is that we've given away far too much power to two things: programs and professionals. We have gotten into the mentality that the right program or the right professional will come riding in on a white horse and save the day. Of course we can use good programs and high-quality professionals, but what we really need is for everyone to get involved in creating safe, resilient, and connected communities for our kids.

Using this more holistic approach to view the challenges our children face will lead us down a different road. In their book *Mobilizing Communities from the Inside Out,* John McKnight and Jodie Kretzman from Northwestern University suggest that if we really want to change a situation, we've got to start by asking a different question. They recommend that rather than beginning by asking, "What are all the problems?" we ask, "What are all our strengths?" When we take this approach, whether it is with our children, our families, our businesses and organizations, or ourselves, we change the equation, tap into creative energy, and identify resources that have been underutilized and unrecognized. At the foundation of this approach is the premise that if we are to effectively deal with our problems, we must first name and claim what is present rather than what is missing, and begin to work with our current assets.

When I am invited into communities to help begin this exciting process, one of the first things I do is put a big piece of blank paper on the wall and ask, "What are all the strengths and resources currently present in our community that support or contribute to the well-being of our youth?" At first, most people do not believe that I would pose such an obvious question. Then major and minor revelations follow. As we start to name and claim our strengths, we affirm our individual and collective worth, identify what we are doing right, and, by so doing, reclaim some of our lost power. In short, we begin to identify exactly how we are making a difference, which is empowering in itself.

Most groups start out tentatively and identify the obvious strengths: Let's see, there are the local youth-serving organizations, the businesses that you can always count on to contribute to youth activities, the DARE officer who will talk to kids about the dangers of using drugs, and the parks and recreation department. Then all of a sudden, the group names a host of individuals and organizations. By the time the list is complete, almost everyone is astonished at how much the community has to offer.

To keep the momentum going, I then ask the group to take the process one step further. "Now," I ask, "think as far outside the usual boxes as you can and name and claim individuals and organizations that are still hidden and that haven't yet been mentioned." After a moment of silence, someone names the piano teacher who has lived down the block for the past thirty years and has taught kids to play the piano whether they wanted to learn or not. Someone else mentions that the local police force has adopted a community policing model in which police officers serve lunch to the kids at school. And another person describes the foster grandparent program, which works closely with local churches and synagogues. And, finally, someone mentions that the PTA or PTO is planning to set up neighborhood watch programs that include kids who "watch out" for each other. Quite often, this process is a catalyst that leads to the suggestion that the group strive to create connections between these community resources. Some groups decide to meet again and to work on methods of increasing the effectiveness of the community's resources.

An activity of this nature is so fundamental and so obvious that it is often overlooked. But how do we begin to shift from a deficit-based to a strength-based way of life on a broader or community-wide scale? When I was in the Midwest, a workshop participant from a community group told me of how they had begun to make this shift happen. They asked young people to nominate an adult who was instrumental in helping them during their lives. At a community awards ceremony, each young person and the nominated adult were invited to meet on stage. The young person presented the adult with a plaque and a heartfelt thanks. Calling this one of the most powerful community moments they could ever remember, participants shed tears, hugged, and affirmed the power of individuals in the community to make a difference.

Sometimes it is useful for groups to describe what they want, rather than define it. For instance, both kids and adults felt respect was one of the things they weren't getting enough of. But if I asked them to define the word *respect,* their eyes would drop. Everybody avoided making eye contact because they didn't want to be put on the spot to define it. Everybody knew what respect was, but defining it was something else. After some trial and error I discovered a much more effective way to get a response. When I asked a group what respect looked like, sounded like, and felt like, hands would shoot up everywhere. Even among disparate groups—gang members, middle school or high school kids—everyone had an immediate response. The process would suddenly come alive—because if we can describe respect, we can create it. Learning to describe what we want and how we can create it is so much more powerful than just defining it. This process can be used across the entire spectrum of our community. Teams I worked with in Indiana spent an hour drawing pictures and writing descriptions of their ideal neighborhood. When the participants presented their product to the larger group, they were almost giddy. Their excitement was reflected in the colorful depiction of their neighborhood, a place where everyone knew everyone else's name, front porches were graced with chairs, neighbors went next door to borrow a couple of eggs, and adults and youth played kickball in the street together. The word *safe* was superimposed over the entire picture. After the activity was finished, a participant said, "At first I thought doing this sounded dumb, but after describing our ideal neighborhood, it all seemed possible. I could actually feel what it could be like to live in a neighborhood that was as connected as the one we created."

A school superintendent learned much about the passion and energy of the students in the high school in his district. These students consistently scored in the top 10 percent on the Scholastic Achievement Test (SAT); naturally, the district was repeatedly lauded for its academic program. He told me that a few years earlier the district had administered a survey to the students to assess a number of items, including school climate. He fully expected the district to be rated far above the national norm, because, he said, "We always do better than everyone else." But when the results were in, he and all at the high school were stunned. The students had actually rated their school climate lower than the national average. The administration's first response was to find fault with the survey rather than to seek a remedy. But after getting through the denial phase, administrators realized that the most important constituency in determining what goes into school climate had never been consulted: the kids! These educators recognized that they had fallen into a habit of doing things "to kids" rather than "with kids."

Much to their credit, they came up with a strategy, convened focus groups consisting of school staff, community members, and students, and invited everyone to describe the type of school climate they wanted, and what it would look like, sound like, and feel like. The students began by saying that the physical atmosphere in the school felt dead, and they wanted to transform it by putting plants everywhere. But for the administrators, a phalanx of red flags went up everywhere: "Who's going to pay for them?" "How are we going to take care of them?" Without missing a beat, the students replied, "We'll take care of it." Like most adults, the ones at this school forgot that kids have all kinds of resources. There are kids whose parents own nurseries, do strategic planning, and facilitate focus groups. Kids have friends who are musicians, computer geniuses, and incredible thespians, all of whose skills can be tapped. Within two weeks, the building was rich with plants donated from some parents who owned a nursery, and teams of students were in place to take care of them. Next, the students requested longer class periods so there would be more in-depth time spent on subject matter (in school jargon this is called block scheduling). In time, this particular district went to block scheduling. In another bold move, the students recommended that breaks between classes be extended from five minutes to fifteen minutes, so they wouldn't have to sprint to a locker, make a hurried pit stop at the bathroom, and then speed off to the next class. On the positive side, the kids said it would give them more opportunities to build relationships and create a stronger community. But again, to the administration red flags went up everywhere. "We've never done it this way," some adults said. "What about control issues?" other adults voiced openly. At last report, the district schools had not yet acted on this recommendation. The issue was just too hot. However, after sharing this story in communities across the country, I have had several people tell me that their high school has gone to ten-minute breaks and they reported a much more relaxed and enjoyable atmosphere.

The great lesson is that they would never even have discussed these topics and many others if they hadn't invited the kids.

In our daily walk through the six circles of life, each of us has numerous opportunities to begin to change or alter our culture. In striking up a conversation with the teenager who carries our groceries to our car, in reviewing our business practices and policies to see if they are friendly to youth and families, and by connecting our kids with the wise elders in our community, we have the power to create a culture that truly cares about our youth. And we might be surprised that in so doing, we will have created a culture that is more nourishing and connected for us all.

As I was making my way through a crowded Minneapolis airport corridor, grateful for once that I did not have to hurry to catch my plane, the sea of people around me suddenly receded, and next to me I saw a child no older than fourteen months, perched on the front edge of a stroller like a sea captain on a ship cutting through the waves, his face to the wind. He radiated an incredible look of joy and exhilaration. I stopped and watched in silent appreciation and awe as this future navigator absorbed all the sights and sounds ahead of him and left a wake of ebullience behind him. As he and his mother bobbed and wove in and out of the traffic, people on the way to their flights sped by him, hardly noticing his ecstatic gaze. I grew a bit concerned as he kept inching farther and farther out of his stroller to maximize the experience. At first I thought he might take a header, but then one of those magical moments in life that last just a microsecond occurred. Maybe he felt my admiring gaze. Or maybe he was just checking out the starboard side of the ship. Suddenly, he turned and made eye contact with me and smiled one of those unbelievably joyful smiles. It was a smile that said, "This is so cool!" And it was a look that said, "Don't worry, the force is with me. I'm in the zone." And in that moment I received one of the profound gifts of a child: a transfer of joy and innocence from his heart to mine. I experienced in a small way what he was experiencing, and as our eyes stayed connected for that magical moment, I smiled back and waved.

Unseen by anyone, this child and I had a sacred exchange that was eternal. It was as though by connecting with him for but a moment I had also connected with all that was good and beautiful in the universe. No amount of research and no survey could ever capture or quantify what had just transpired. In my opinion, I had come close to God. Just then, his mom banked toward one of the gates and I watched as this future sea captain inched up a bit more on his stroller to see what awaited at this exotic port of call. As I continued toward my gate, contemplating my good fortune, a dad suddenly emerged in front of me with a newborn cast over his shoulder: Staring at me, right at eye level, were two of the biggest, bluest eyes I had ever seen. This was my lucky day.

Throughout the six circles of our lives, experiences like these are available to all of us if we shift our attention and focus to include our most valuable resource, our kids. The gift kids bring to activities across the circle of life are joy, enthusiasm, honesty, and hope for the future. All of us can help nourish these beautiful gifts in whatever circles of life we find ourselves.

TWO

The First Circle:
The Individual

*What mean ye, fellow citizens, that ye turn every stone
to scrape wealth together, and take so little care of your children,
to whom ye must one day relinquish all?*

—SOCRATES

In the first circle of community, all of us have numerous opportunities to make a big difference in the lives of kids. Whether we're carpenters or classroom aides, parents or stockbrokers, if we are attentive during each of our own daily walks through life, we will discover we have numerous opportunities to alter the culture by building relationships with young people.

When we take action in this first circle of community, it ripples subtly through all the other circles of life. Action in our immediate circle is very personal, sometimes incredibly spontaneous, and always from the heart. We start by doing the small things and then continue by seizing opportunities wherever they present themselves. From acknowledging the young people we pass on the street to shooting some hoops with kids who live on our neighborhood block, these small acts begin to alter the environment around us.

The exciting part of the first circle is that it is so immediate. We don't have to enlist the help of anyone else. We don't have to wait for programs, funding, or permission. We don't have to have a special degree. As I work with community members across North America who want to create a caring community for their kids, the very first secret we talk about is the power and importance of "showing up." While I was in Rapid City, South Dakota, conducting a workshop entitled "Creating a Healthy, Caring Community for Our Kids," I began by sharing one of my favorite Woody Allen quotes—that "75 percent of winning is just showing up." At the break, a member of the Lakota tribe that had sent representatives to the workshop pulled me aside and said: "In our community, before we convene a tribal meeting, one of the first things we do is a quick 'check-in' to see if everyone has really shown up or not." He explained to me that they believed that just because someone showed up physically, it didn't necessarily mean they were there mentally, emotionally, or spiritually. He continued by telling me, "If someone comes to a meeting, we need them to be there as fully as possible. If not, why come?" As he was talking, I was thinking about all the times I had sat in a classroom, attended a seminar, or gone to church being about only 49 percent there. I thanked him for this insight, and as we returned to the workshop, I realized that this meant me as well. There is just one great secret to being successful in the first circle. The secret lies in the power of showing up—starting with small acts and moving on to giving kids tasks that will make them feel trusted, valued, and recognized.

❁

SHOWING UP

When I was working as a classroom aide in an elementary school, I discovered early on that if I played kickball or jumped rope with the kids, I was a hero. If I sat down and ate lunch with them, I became a legend. If I talked with them about their lives, I was the stuff of which epics were made.

The power of truly "showing up" in a kid's life is awesome. It means much more than being there physically. It also means showing up psychologically. It means listening, really listening, whether we like what we hear or not. It means knowing these kids are going to make mistakes and being there for them when they do. It means keeping our promises and making them a priority in our lives. But most of all, showing up means loving children unconditionally and remembering that we were all kids once, hoping an adult would love us enough to truly show up in our lives.

Those who show up in the lives of our kids are our real community heroes. They usually receive little thanks and recognition, but these are the people who are fashioning and setting in place the building blocks of generations to come.

❁   THE AMAZING MRS. TINTERELLI

In a small neighborhood in Calgary, Alberta, Canada, to get from one side to the other you had to take a shortcut that went right through Mrs. Tinterelli's backyard.

Mrs. Tinterelli could have been angry at all the trespassers.

After all, there was a six-inch dirt path that cut right through her lawn. Instead of getting upset when she saw one of the kids coming down the path, Mrs. Tinterelli would motion for him to come to her back steps, where she had cookies waiting. Sometimes they'd talk. Other times the kids would give her a big smile and a thank you and continue on their way. On hot summer nights it was not uncommon to see Mrs. Tinterelli sitting on her back porch listening to one of the kids pour out his heart to her. She laughed and cried with all the kids who came around her back porch. It was a place of safety, where unconditional love was freely offered and received. An interesting phenomenon grew out of these incredible relationships. When fall arrived, her leaves were always magically raked and bagged. When winter came with a vengeance, her walk was always shoveled. And when summer arrived, her lawn was always mowed.

When Mrs. Tinterelli moved to a retirement home, the kids couldn't get used to her not being there. They lingered around her backyard for months, hoping that she'd somehow reappear with her plateful of cookies and her gifts of the heart. Mrs. Tinterelli left a legacy that touched countless lives.

❀ PLAY SOME BALL—CATCH A KID

"I was working with a family that had all kinds of problems," said a social worker from a small Montana town. "After spending time with them, I saw how the impact of all their issues had affected their nine-year-old son. To get attention, he would spin around the living room on the carpet, say inappropriate things, and then push everybody away who tried to come near. One day when I was about to leave, I decided to take a risk. I asked the boy if he wanted to play catch with me sometime. Looking at me some-what disdainfully, he shook his head and said, 'No!' over and over. I told him I'd be back at two o'clock the next day. He told me not to bother. I didn't know what to expect, but the following after-noon, as I crept down his street in my car, I caught sight of him hiding in the bushes next to his house. When I pulled into their driveway and got out of the car with a mitt, he suddenly emerged from the bushes beaming. Draped around his arm were two gloves and a ball. He was more than ready to go. He was ecstatic."

❀ THE BULLY

After trying everything, including time outs, calling home, and keeping him after class, a teacher told me she was just about to give up on the sixth-grade bully who was terrorizing the school. After all, nothing she did to try to correct his behavior worked. Not want-ing to give up on him, she decided, "I've tried all the conventional ways; maybe I'll try one that just makes sense, [since] what he really wants," she thought, "is attention." With that in mind, she called up the boy's mom and asked her if she could take him to a movie on Saturday night. The mom was so stunned by the question that it was followed by a long period of silence; she was crying. After a few moments, she composed herself and said shakily, "Are you sure you want to take him?" In the back of her mind, the teacher was think-ing "Maybe not," but she nevertheless said that she was sure.

Standing on the boy's doorstep at 6:45 P.M., the teacher didn't know what to expect. But when the door opened, her jaw dropped. There was Mom, smiling from ear to ear, and when the bully stepped out from behind her, he had on a white shirt and a tie, his hair was slicked back, and he was ready to go. The teacher was further confounded when the boy sprinted ahead and opened the car door for her. Watching all this proudly from the living room window was Mom. Nothing else miraculous happened that night, but the teacher realized something important about the boy. At school he had a role that everyone expected of him. Sure, he helped create it, and it wasn't very positive, but he lived up to it every time he could. Out of school, a different dimension emerged. He was like all kids. He was looking for love and recognition.

When school started Monday morning, he was still the school bully, but in her classroom he had become the number one helper. He followed her around everywhere, trying to build that relationship. He still did some dumb stuff, but she had seen his other side, and that was something he liked.

I was sharing the story with a group in the Midwest, and a man in his forties sauntered up to me at a break and said, "You know, I was just like that kid when I was growing up. I had a lot of anger and took it out on everyone around me. After a while, that's who I thought I was. When I was in my midtwenties, my life was so messed up I was on the verge of committing suicide. But you know something? I had a teacher just like that one you mentioned. She saw something in me that I couldn't see, and when I was about to kill myself, I thought about her, and I decided that if she could see something positive, maybe it was really there. Since that moment, my life has totally changed, and now I work with troubled kids and I try to help them see the 'other side' of themselves."

❀   THE POWER OF BEING THERE

A workshop participant told me a great story she had read about the power of being present in a young person's life: One day a woman's son came to her and said, "Mom, let's go outside and shoot baskets. My job is to shoot the ball. Your job is to watch and then say, 'How wonderful!'"

FIVE EASY WAYS YOU CAN MAKE
A KID FEEL IMPORTANT

1. Whenever you encounter a child, take note of a detail in his appearance—an interesting haircut, a T-shirt logo, a pleasant smile—and comment (kindly) on it.
2. Whatever a child who comes to your door is selling— buy!
3. Create a special signal that you give to children you regularly encounter in your neighborhood (pull your ear, for example, or salute).
4. Remember names and use them.
5. At the grocery store, compliment the child in your line loudly enough so his or her parent can hear.

❀

SMALL ACTS

Perhaps one of the biggest mistakes we make today is to believe that in order to create change, we have to do something huge. If we have to do something huge, we feel overwhelmed and do nothing at all. It's nat-

---

ural, then, to do nothing at all. A friend of mine, after reading the headlines about the latest school shootings and all the lousy statistics of what's happening in our kids' lives, announced, "I'm thinking about creating a new bumper sticker that reads: 'Warning: Statistics and Headlines May Cause Depression.'"

❀ EVERYONE PLAYS

My dad coached every sport. The funny thing about it was he didn't really know a whole lot about football, baseball, or basketball. But he had something few coaches had. He had a remarkable philosophy: "Everyone plays." You knew that if you were on his team, you would get in the game. Kids everywhere wanted to be on "Easy Ed's" team. One day, when I was older, I learned one of the reasons my dad did all this. Growing up in Minneapolis, my dad was always the last kid chosen for every team, and he decided he would do whatever he could so that wouldn't happen to other kids. Ironically, not only did he win lots of championships, but he became somewhat of a Little League legend. I really didn't understand his impact and his legacy until I grew up. Whenever I ran into some old teammates or kids who had played for him, the first question they asked was not "How are you?" but rather "How's your dad?" They didn't talk about winning games; they talked about what a great guy he was.

❀ GREETING AND MEETING

"When I retire from the juvenile justice system I want to be the greeter at Wal-Mart!" a community member from Indianapolis blurted out. After we all howled, she good-heartedly said, "There's a reason for it. I really enjoy meeting people and connecting with them, and I could get paid to do it!" Sobering up a bit, we wondered aloud, "Why does Wal-Mart have a greeter?" The answers and the connection to what we were doing were immediately apparent. The greeter builds relationships and may track in some way who is at the store. And some customers may decide to shop at Wal-Mart because they know Muriel, who will be saying "Hi" to them when they arrive.

What's the connection? Suppose we had greeters at parks and recreation departments, at malls, at schools, at all places kids hang out? One school district I was working with started having high school students at middle schools and elementary schools to greet the kids. Another school considered having parents and senior citizens greet high schoolers each morning. One mom said aloud, "Maybe if we have friendly adults and older kids greeting kids at the doors to our schools, we won't have to turn to metal detectors."

❀   THE EYES OF THE BEHOLDER

"While I was watching my son's high school basketball game," a mom from Sundance, Wyoming said, "I kept hearing a boy about the age of twelve cheering for my son. 'Go, Tom, go,' he kept yelling. 'Attaboy, Tom,' he called out again and again. Finally, I made my way down to the boy and said, 'I keep hearing you cheering for Tom. Do you know him?' The boy looked up at me sheepishly and replied, 'No, but I really like his haircut!' Chuckling, I inquired, 'Would you like to meet Tom after the game?' Wide-eyed, the boy nodded and said incredulously, 'Could I?' When the game concluded, the boy and I trotted out onto the court, and I introduced Tom to him. Tom was very gracious and spent some time talking sports with his new-found fan. The boy was awestruck; my son was a hero. As I reflected upon the experience, I realized how none of this would've happened if I hadn't approached the young man. It only took a few minutes, but it created a memory that would last for some time."

❀ THE POWER OF NAMES

When I taught school, I tried to acknowledge, by name, every kid I saw in the hallway, at a sports event, or in the community. I remember bumping into three kids one day after school. I said "Hi" to two of them, but I couldn't think of the third kid's name. He said, "Hey, how about me?" They saw that I was bewildered and embarrassed, and finally he got me off the hook when he laughed and said, "My name is Travis, but I'm just visiting!" I chuckled and said, "Hey Travis!" and we headed on our separate ways. I had a similar experience when I went to a movie with some friends. The theater was downtown and we had to park several blocks away. After the movie ended, it was late, and as we were walking back to the car, we came around a corner and almost ran into a group of guys who were smoking and huddled together to keep warm. Our adrenaline levels went up a bit, because this was not a part of town that was considered safe. I glanced around the circle and recognized one of the kids who had a history of trouble in school. I didn't know how I would be received but remarkably he smiled and said, as though he was actually happy to see me, "Hey, Mr. V." Relieved, I replied, "What are you guys doing out in the cold?" We both laughed a little uneasily, but at the moment, any tension dissolved immediately. "You guys watch out for us down here, OK?" I said as we headed toward our car. "No problem," he said assuredly. Discussing it later, my friends and I agreed we actually felt safer knowing they were there! By acknowledging their presence, we were helping to create our own safety zone.

❀ OPEN HOUSE

Every Friday night, a mom from Waterloo, Iowa told me, she holds an open house for her kids and any of their friends who want to come over. "There just weren't any safe places for these kids to go," she said. "So I figured they could come here!" They make pizza together, watch videos, and talk. She says that for the most part she just listens and helps them sort out their thoughts. At times, this informal event is attended by five kids, while other nights as many as forty come. Sometimes her own kids aren't even there! But every Friday night, she shows up and is available to love and hold these kids in times of great need. As I listened to her talk, I could feel her incredible love for these kids. "Kids are like heat-seeking missiles looking for adults who really care about them," she concluded. And in her they had found one big, receptive target. Her gift to the community is immeasurable, the cost minimal, the benefits immense. And she didn't need a grant to pull it off.

❀ REALITY CHECK

"Yeah, all this sounds great," said a weary juvenile justice officer as we were discussing the importance of adults reaching out to youth, "but what about the predators and molesters out there, who will just use this approach for themselves? Doesn't this just give them an open invitation to prey on kids?" The whole group fell quiet. He was right. We spent the next half hour discussing this very important topic, and finally agreed that predators and molesters operate most freely when there are huge gaps between the circles of support within a child's life, when no one is around to see what is happening and to intervene. We decided that when we, as caring and committed adults, help reconnect and restore these circles of support, we go a long way toward shutting out these predators and molesters. We also agreed that two adults should be present at all times when kids are involved in extracurricular activities, and that background checks should be made on all adults who want to work with kids. Perking up, the juvenile justice officer said, "You know, most law enforcement agencies will do those background checks for free or for a nominal cost." He continued, "My experience has been that, by taking a little time, it can save a lot of pain later on."

❁

FEELING TRUSTED, VALUED, AND RECOGNIZED

When I was in the first grade, I had the awesome task of taking the attendance sheet from my classroom all the way down to the administrative office. I still recall how quiet the halls were, how I avoided the intimidating sixth-grade lockers, and how large the porcelain drink-

ing fountain was that I would stop at along the way. I remember how important I felt walking into the main office where all the adults were, and the feeling of pride I had when I placed the attendance list on the counter.

When I share this memory with groups, lightbulbs start going on everywhere. People become extremely animated and eager to share their own childhood experiences: being responsible for keeping the wood fire going in a one-room schoolhouse, being on safety patrol and wearing the special safety patrol belt, driving a tractor on a farm, cleaning the erasers outside the classroom (and returning covered with chalk), being responsible for the class while a teacher had to leave, playing a solo at a middle-school concert, feeding the pet lizard, babysitting, being asked by an adult to help coach a team, being in charge of a camp store that consisted of a folding table and some candy and pencils, being trusted with the keys to the gym.

By trusting our kids to contribute in small, helpful ways, we prepare them to participate, take responsibility, and play meaningful roles in the decades to come. By recognizing kids not only for getting good grades and other achievements, but for their efforts and for who they are, we are giving them a great gift.

❀ THE DESIRE TO BE IMPORTANT

"I get kids coming to me for all kinds of reasons," a school secretary who worked on a native reserve in Canada said to me, "but only recently did I discover what an impact I can have on them. After all," she continued somewhat self-consciously, "I wasn't trained to work with kids. I don't have a degree! One boy who was considered the 'school loser' started coming by my desk and asking if he could help me. Seeing he needed a friend, I came up with all kinds of chores he could do, and we'd talk just about everything.

"One day, I told him how I missed my own children because they had left home and gone to school. I told him there was a big gap in my life that they used to fill. Looking up from his task, he said to me so earnestly, 'I bet you're glad that you have me!' Startled by his response and seeing the expectant look on his face I replied, 'Oh yes, as a matter of fact, I think you were sent to me.' As I spoke those words," she concluded, "a little smile appeared on his face, and then he looked down and continued with his job." Reflecting for a moment, she then said, "I wouldn't have exchanged that moment for anything."

❀ THE CRUSADER

"When I was a kid," a guy in his forties told me, "for Halloween I decided I wanted to be a Crusader. I had seen a movie about them and couldn't think of anything more masculine. My mom and I worked for weeks on my costume. When the big night rolled around, I had a cardboard sword covered with tinfoil at my side, big boots, and a sheet with a huge, red cross on it. As my friends and I went door to door, I thought everyone was duly impressed, as I was met with smiles and nods. I figured everyone recognized a Crusader when they saw one! However, toward the end of the night, my bubble burst and I realized why I was getting all these mixed looks. A lady opened the door, and, when she saw me, she called out to her husband, 'George, come here and look! It's a boy dressed as a Red Cross nurse.' I was acknowledged," he said laughing, "but not the way I wanted to be!"

FIVE GREAT WAYS TO SHOW YOU CARE

1. Be the kind of adult you hope children will become. Model acts of kindness every day: open doors, be courteous, be forgiving, be giving.
2. Go beyond saying "Hi" to kids; ask "How's school, [soccer, etc.]?"
3. Be home on Halloween and give out memorable treats.
4. Keep a joke or riddle in your pocket for younger kids.
5. Lighten up with teens. (They think adults are much too serious.)

❀

KIDS AS RESOURCES AND PARTICIPANTS: NOT THE ENEMY!

As I talk with teenagers across America, one thing is evident: They do not feel valued. Many feel as if they're the enemy. Black kids have told me how humiliating it is to walk down their neighborhood streets and see people in cars at stop signs and stoplights check to make sure their windows are rolled up and their doors locked; white kids in rural Ohio have told me they're not allowed to shop in certain stores. Do you believe teens are dangerous? One big question we all have to ask ourselves is: "What do I really believe about our kids?" Sometimes, what we think we believe can be challenged in the most unexpected places.

❀ THE PURPLE-HAIRED WAKE-UP CALL

I had only forty-five minutes to get through customs and to my plane at the packed Vancouver, B.C., International Airport. Standing ahead of me was a teenager with purple hair, a pierced nose, ripped tennis shoes, and low-slung jeans. As I contemplated whether to ask him if I could go ahead of him, I was suddenly struck by my lack of courage. I was intimidated by this kid! Finally, after about twenty minutes had passed, I made eye contact and said, "Excuse me, but I have only about fifteen minutes to check in, get through customs, and catch my plane. Unless you have an earlier flight, do you mind if I go ahead?"

Without a moment's hesitation he responded, "No problem," and then proceeded to scoop up my bags and move them to the front of the line. Amazed, I said, "Thanks," and while I waited for the next available agent, I asked him where he was headed. His eyes grew wide and his voice excited as he replied, "I'm off to Alaska for the whole summer where I'm going to be a counselor at a Bible camp!"

Making a beeline toward customs, I laughed the whole way as I thought, "I should have asked him what the denomination of his church was!" As I reflected upon the experience, I recalled the time when I was a few years older than he; I had hair down to my shoulders and wore overalls and an African bead bracelet draped around my waist. "The costumes have changed," I thought, "but teenagers still have the same basic feelings and needs."

✿ SMOKE BUT NO FIRE

"During the school year," boomed a voice from the front row at a seminar, "my daily walk would always take me by a group of teenagers who hung out on the corner across from the school, smoking. I used to make this wide circle around them, hoping there would be no trouble, because I didn't know what to expect. But after hearing how important it was to build relationships with kids in our daily lives, I decided that on my next walk I would say hello to them as I passed by. I can't say I wasn't a little nervous, because I was. But I was determined to make contact with them.

"On the day I decided to do this, I almost chickened out. But when I got a couple of feet away from them, I cleared my throat, and although it must have surprised them as much as it did me, I let out a weak hello and a forced smile. About half a block later the adrenaline was still pumping. But as I continued, I realized that I hadn't been beaten up, accosted, or robbed, and so I decided to keep it up. After the first week a few of them looked at me and started saying, 'Hi' back. After the second week, I slowed down and started exchanging some small talk. At the end of the third week, they actually invited me to hang out on the corner with them! Now I stop and talk with them all the time. And you know the first question they ask if I miss my walk one day? It's 'Where were you?'"

✿ ATTENTION AT ANY COST

During a workshop, we were listing all the positives that kids get out of organized sports and activities. We charted how these activities allow youth to play meaningful roles, have a sense of belonging, and meet challenges; they have a support group that sets goals and objectives, they have rites of passage and older mentors—they even get mentioned in the newspaper once in a while. At the break, a guy in his forties from Oakland, California, came up to me and said, "You know, I'm a gang prevention coordinator, and what we just listed is everything that kids in a gang desire! You know," he said, a little confounded, "we can see these kids who join gangs coming from a million miles away, but we're so busy hauling kids out of the river after they've fallen in, we don't spend enough time upstream—showing them how to swim. These kids could go either way. We need to get to them earlier." At that moment, it all seemed so simple—working at the source, not after the fact, is one of the important answers.

THE BIG MOTIVATOR

A principal at a Baltimore, Maryland, inner-city middle school told me that when they did a locker check one day, they discovered a locker that had stacks and stacks of Monopoly money all carefully rubber-banded together. Having never seen this before, the principal called the two boys who used this locker into her office. After a few moments, the boys fessed up. They told the principal, "This is how all the drug dealers handle their money. We're just practicing!" Astounded, the principal said it took her a few minutes to recover. "So, you two want to make money?" she inquired. "Yeah," each responded. The next day, the principal's stockbroker from Dean Witter Investments came to the school to teach the kids how to get the adrenaline rush they were experiencing through their "drug dealing" by investing money in the stock market. The kids started out picking stocks with Monopoly money and tracking their "buys." After hearing the story, a community member gave them a generous gift of five hundred dollars, and the young men are now "dealing" in a new way. They follow the market. They're studying commerce, math, and the law and are using their innate talents in legal ways. Now the kids have stopped listening to the local drug dealers and have started listening when their investment broker talks!

❈

SPECIAL KIDS IN SPECIAL COMMUNITIES

Quite often in discussions about valuing our kids, we leave out a whole spectrum of youth: kids with physical, mental, or emotional disabilities. These kids are our kids, too, and because we are getting more accustomed to including them in day-to-day activities, we are beginning to learn of the incredible gifts they give to our community—gifts that often lie dormant, waiting to be discovered.

Mother Teresa and her Sisters of Charity opened a home for children with disabilities. They asked mothers and fathers who had children with autism, cerebral palsy, Down's syndrome, and other disabilities if they would like the children to live in the new home where they would be cared for. Many of the parents, overwhelmed by just finding enough to eat on a daily basis, were very grateful for the help, but one mother, when asked if she wanted the sisters to care for her child, looked at them in horror. Shaking her head back and forth vigorously, she said emphatically, "Oh, I could never give you this child. You see, she is my teacher of love."

✿ SPECIAL KIDS BRING SPECIAL CHALLENGES

Our firstborn son had a horrendous birth. Stuck in the birth canal for some time, he fought for oxygen and his life. When he finally emerged, his head was a bloody mass, but he was alive. Nick spent days in the intensive recovery unit, and when we finally took him home, we thought the horrible days were behind us. But in the following months, Nick's constant crying, his resistance to being held, and his chronic ear infections left us exhausted. We were encouraged as he got older and remarkable golden curls appeared on his head; he was an uncommonly handsome kid.

But still we were troubled by many of his reactions to the world; for example, when we put him on the grass, he would scream as if tiny razor blades were cutting into him. His language skills were delayed, but we thought he'd catch up. He insisted on having everything in his own perfect order and we would joke about the wrath that would fall upon us if we dared move one of his toy cars from its perfect place. We didn't know what was developmentally natural and normal for kids his age.

But one day it hit us hard. He was in a gymnastics class for four-year-olds, and all the parents had assembled to watch what their young ones had learned. One at a time, child after child somersaulted to the applause and delight of their parents, and when it was Nick's turn we were ready to respond just the same way. But he just ran down the gymnastic pads, smiling, and then spun and turned and ran back into line. My wife and I looked at each other in total shock. "Still," we reasoned, "he's just a bit behind!"

But a few years later we were confronted again. He was scoring several grade levels lower than the other kids and he was becoming more reclusive. Soon, a diagnosis was made: he was autistic. His autism was considered mild, but it nonetheless hit us like a thunderbolt. We had been so good at denial. I'll never forget watching him wired to an electroencephalograph and watching the lines go flat. "That," the doctor explained to me, "is a seizure." One doctor stunned us when he said Nick should probably be institutionalized. That was totally unacceptable.

That was years ago. Nick, now twenty-one, graduated from high school on time with lots of help from some really caring teachers. He wants to be a radio broadcaster! For countless nights, we've sat and listened to his self-generated radio and Academy Awards shows. It's all paid off. He's now enrolling in an Internet broadcasting school, and one day you just might hear him, featuring his favorite show tunes, on NPR!

❀ CHUCKY'S STORY

"When I was in elementary school," a mom began, "I lived across the street from a family with six kids. Their house was filled with toys and 'stuff,' and they seemed different from other families. The key to their special situation was that their fourth kid was what people then called a 'retard.' His name was Chucky and he had been labeled 'borderline trainable.' The professionals told his parents he wouldn't live very long, that he had epilepsy, and that they should put him in an institution; but his parents wouldn't do that. They just stuck him in the middle of their family and acted like everything was normal.

"We could tell when Chucky was coming down the street because he walked like a drunk. He looked kind of goofy and gave the whole family a less-than-perfect image. When Chucky got lost, we all searched for him. When Chucky fell down, we all picked him up. When Chucky got teased, we all stood up for him.

"We didn't know it then, but Chucky gave us all a common cause. He was not only a part of his family but a part of us, too. He redefined 'retard' for us and made us compassionate for other humans. And we redefined Chucky. This 'borderline trainable' kid went to elementary, junior high, and high school. He took cooking classes and became the manager of the varsity football team. He went on family vacations, met the governor, and learned, with the help of his family and community, to live in the world.

"In 1977 I married Chucky's brother. Chucky couldn't come to the wedding because he was in Colorado competing in the Special Olympics! So now that less-than-perfect family that includes a retarded kid was *my* family! How could that happen? How could I *choose* to be a part of such a family? Well, here's how: While learning love for and acceptance of Chucky, his family learned love for and acceptance of all people. While tracking the woods in northern Michigan searching for the frost-bitten, lost-in-the-night little boy, they learned not to care that he teetered when he walked. They only hoped that he lived.

"At Thanksgiving we will all sit around the table. Chucky will tell us over and over again about his job at the restaurant and about his girlfriend. He'll comment on football and politics and on some movie he's seen a dozen times. Chucky turned forty this year. He still teeters when he walks. And once in a while he gets lost, but he has never seen the inside of an institution and he has experienced more of life than many forty-year-olds. He has a loving family whom he has richly rewarded with his life. We give thanks for all the love we have learned from this special person."

FIVE THOUGHTFUL WAYS TO
HELP SPECIAL KIDS

1. Acknowledge and engage special kids; don't withdraw or pull away.
2. Introduce your children to kids with impairments; help make your own kids comfortable with them.
3. Raise your special child as normally as possible (chores, discipline, etc.).
4. If you have a special kid, strive to build personal relationships with the professionals who diagnose and help them understand your pain.
5. If you're a professional in this field, throw out the technical jargon and really relate at a heart-to-heart level to parents who are going through a difficult time.

❀

ALL KIDS HAVE UNIQUE GIFTS

In this highly toxic culture, whether our kids are labeled "gifted and talented," "at risk," or "special," they all need lots of attention. What they really need is for someone to believe in them, help them identify their gifts, and then provide opportunities for these gifts to be expressed.

In this first circle of community, we begin by taking small steps that in turn will ripple across the web of life and through all of life. At first it may not seem as though we are making progress because we may not see anything tangible. But there will be changes. In the words of the philosopher Pascal, "The entire ocean is affected by a pebble."

THE TOP TEN WAYS TO SAVE A KID: IN THE PERSONAL CIRCLE

1. Love them and show it (and stop at every lemonade stand).
2. Identify a gift you have to give children and share it: a listening heart, woodworking skills, fondness of baking, love of outdoor sports—you name it.
3. Schedule time with your own kids (in your appointment book or on your calendar).
4. Tell your kids stories about your own life and about the wonder of their birth.
5. Compliment a young person in front of other adults.
6. Use situations to teach and affirm, not to condemn or criticize.
7. Go out of your way to meet your children's friends.
8. Play a game with a young person.
9. Listen to kids' music and ask about the lyrics and the band.
10. Accept nose rings as a fact of life (you'll live longer).

THREE

The Second Circle:
The Family

The strength of a nation is derived from the integrity of its homes.
—CONFUCIUS

In the house that I grew up in, we had a ritual that revolved around the shower, which was upstairs. Before you hopped into it, you'd call downstairs to alert the whole family. Why? If anyone anywhere in the house flushed a toilet or turned on a faucet, your shower would immediately be scalding hot. I can still remember being a victim of the plumbing and leaping into the shower curtain or hugging the white metal side of the shower stall if someone downstairs committed this cardinal sin. But I also remember that if I was really mad at my older brother, I knew exactly how to get back at him. I'd time the flush for just the right moment and then chuckle when I heard the anguished scream come from the bathroom.

The plumbing was a real pain, but because of it we had to communicate with each other. If we didn't, we suffered immediate and unbearable consequences. Today, most modern homes come equipped with lots of hi-tech devices, and we are communicating less and less. Kids as well as parents have computers, phones, and televisions in their own rooms. Everyone in the house runs on a different schedule and attends different events. In some families, parents and kids may not connect for days.

When we have a "disconnect" like this at a grassroots level, activities like eating dinner together as a family becomes an exception rather than the rule. To many, connecting with extended families becomes a distant and impossible dream. But there are opportunities everywhere to connect with our kids. It may seem impossible with changing family dynamics, sibling rivalries, and parents who lead stress-filled lives, but it isn't. Reconnecting our families takes some common sense, creativity, and, most of all, commitment—no matter what size, shape, or configuration of the family.

❁

EXTENDING THE FAMILY

If you grew up in the 1940s, 1950s, or 1960s, chances are your extended family was nearby. You may recall big family events—grandparents, aunts, uncles, and cousins all crowding into one living room, on a small front porch, or in the yard to celebrate a holiday or someone's birthday. Maybe you had a weird uncle that no one talked much about but who handed out dollar bills whenever he saw you. Perhaps there was a cool aunt who treated you like an adult, really listened to you, and encouraged you to follow your dreams. Your grandfather may have taken you fishing. With these unique characters you consumed lavish Sunday dinners, played fierce rounds of Ping-Pong and horseshoes, or maybe watched a relative who drank too much. Life was far from perfect, but the circle of support was in clear view. The essence of this circle is summed up when a little girl is asked by her parents, "What's the special word you need to use to get what you want?" and the little girl shouts, "Grandpa!"

The extended family has all but disappeared. Stephen Glenn of Capabilities, Inc., reports that in 1950, 50 percent of all American homes had grandparents in or near them. Today, fewer than 10 percent of parents live close enough to their parents to take advantage of their support in the toughest of all jobs—being a parent. As parents, we have to be creative and think of ways in which we can connect our children to their family histories and distant relatives; it's up to us to generate networks of support to serve as proxies for those we used to have with our extended families.

※   TELLING THE FAMILY STORY

Many of us probably know more about the fictional lives of families on some television series than we know about our own. But these vital histories need to be told and retold. The desire to be Americans may have caused some immigrants to purposely discard their precious family histories. Yet these stories of emigration, hope, strife, war, love, and accomplishment are powerful ways of staying connected to our families. They also help us to define who we are.

In *Stories: The Family Legacy,* Richard Stone poses questions that can help us begin to embrace the past. He suggests we research our family names, accounts of the first settlers in our family, our grandparents' histories, family legends, and stories about eccentric relatives and our own births. Some of today's most popular Web sites deal with family genealogies, family names, family trees, and the stories of families that migrated to America.

You can keep the spirit of your family alive by telling endearing stories about:

- your family's arrival in this country
- how your kids' grandparents met
- the births of your kids
- a dumb thing you did when you were growing up
- a wacky thing you and your best friend did in high school
- how much tennis shoes and jeans cost when you were growing up
- where your family used to go on vacation
- an eccentric uncle or aunt

❁ THE FAMILY HISTORY

"One night," a gentleman of about my age volunteered, "around the dinner table during a big family reunion, one of my great-aunts—who probably had had one more glass of wine than usual—started talking about our family. Once she got going, everyone joined in, and my sister and I listened with our jaws dropping onto the table. Suddenly, stories we had never heard were being shared, and our pretty, Teflon-coated family all of a sudden burst into this incredible soap opera! There was the story about our great-grandparents who sacrificed everything to come to America to start life over. And I learned I had two great-uncles who fought in World War I—and one of them married a French girl and their first child died! My great-aunt told us about her black-sheep sister who chose a life in the theater, which was scandalous at the time, and our very quiet uncle opened up and talked about his exploits during World War II." Then, pausing, he said, "My grandmother told us that Grandpa, who is now deceased, was so shy, she had to kiss him first. 'I had a few things to teach him,' she said, as we all howled. That night we laughed and cried together as a family. It was like we were rediscovering part of ourselves that had been lost for a long, long time."

✿ THE "INTENDED" EXTENDED FAMILY

"I was really worried about the lack of aunts, uncles, and grandparents in my kids' lives," a single mom from Nebraska said, "so I approached some of my most trusted friends and asked them if they'd be willing to play the role of surrogate relative in the life of my kids. I knew I was asking a lot, but several said yes. We held big family dinners to bring them all together; a bond was slowly built between us all. The adults fell in love with my kids and would call informally just to chat. They also showed up for birthday parties, holidays, and other special events in my children's lives." Sighing, she said, "They were there when a crisis occurred, and we celebrated, laughed, and cried together during tough times. What was so wonderful is that I think the adults benefitted as much as my kids . . . they relearned how to play catch, fly a kite, and receive lots of love in return."

❀

WORKING TOGETHER

To bring our families back together, we need to start planning to make it happen. Many of us have come to realize it won't happen magically. We've got to get out our Day-Timers and calendars, schedule family meetings, and start blocking out games, plays, and special times to spend with our kids.

❀ EVERYTHING YOU NEED TO KNOW
ABOUT BEING A PARENT

A group of parents at a workshop on the East Coast came up with an impressive list of small but significant acts that are part of being a parent: Read to your children; start when they are infants and don't stop. Tell them stories about your life. Listen, really listen. Don't be afraid to cry in front of them when you are happy or sad. Don't tell them all your problems—remember, they are kids. Acknowledge your mistakes and admit being wrong. Apologize when you make a mistake. Know that they will make mistakes and don't be surprised when they do. Set rules, consequences, curfews, and expectations, but trust them to do the right thing. Tell them how happy you are to have them in your life. Always show up at performances and parent-teacher conferences. Bake something special with them. Prepare your child's favorite dish when you eat alone with that child. Don't overreact to a messy room. Take your children out to breakfast and talk to them. Always display artwork on the refrigerator. Create a secret signal that says "I love you." Never miss a chance to say, "I love you." Don't be embarrassing at your kids' events. Act as a chauffeur for your kids and their friends. And listen! If you really listen, you can learn a lot. Keep a list of your kids' friends' phone numbers next to the phone in case you need to contact them. Make your house a place your children feel comfortable bringing their friends to. And remember, they really do want us to speak up, intervene, or call them on behaviors that are out of line, and let them know that trust is learned.

❀   TOTAL FAMILY INVOLVEMENT

"Every Friday night, over twenty years ago," said a friend, "all seven kids in our family and our parents would gather for a family meeting. With our dad as the self-appointed chairman of the family board, we learned *Robert's Rules of Order,* discussed how to lower light bills, and sometimes ended the meeting with a talent show." Laughing, she continued, "My dad would even make special guest appearances as Mr. McGillicudy. He would knock on the door, and each of the kids would take turns greeting him, taking his coat, and showing him a seat! We would end each family meeting with a quote that sounded like it came straight out of *Poor Richard's Almanac.* Some of them I remember are, 'Home is where you hang your hat.' 'If you hoot with the owls at night, you can't soar with the eagles in the morning.' 'Let's have happy talk at the dinner table.'"

Showing me some of the minutes from the "board" meetings, we both cracked up when we read entries such as: "Bobby is drinking from the toilet again." "Daddy says we shouldn't tell others our family secrets." "Everyone will receive 1 cent for trying new food."

"Tom says everyone should be assessed 2 cents an hour for leaving lights on." "Kathy had a problem about Jeanne's attitude doing dishes."

The life of their family was chronicled along the way. The experiences and memories were always waiting to be read by future generations.

❀ CREATING FAMILY HARMONY

"I was working with a family that had a lot of problems," a family counselor told me. "They argued constantly, and the whole house was filled with tension. I decided to start small, and suggested that they come up with just one positive thing they had going for them. After about an hour, they finally came up with one: They all agreed that they loved to sing. As I left, their assignment was to agree on a song they all liked and that they would sing at my next visit.

"One week later, when I walked through the door, the family broke into an incredible rendition of Otis Redding's 'Respect.' When they finished, I was astonished when they gave each other high-fives, followed by a group hug with me in the middle! Finally, after we all calmed down, they said it was one of the best experiences they had ever had as a family. Sometimes," she mused, "we all need to just have fun together and discover what we share in common, not what keeps up apart."

SEVEN EASY WAYS TO RECONNECT FAMILIES

1. Identify family strengths and build on them.
2. Schedule nights of the week so that the whole family eats dinner together.
3. Have family rituals, celebrate with special foods, songs, and trips.
4. Hold a family reunion and talk about the exploits of family members.
5. Create a home environment in which your kids' friends feel welcome. (You can learn a lot.)
6. Send out a newsletter with holiday greetings, updating family members.
7. When possible, let your kids have the self-satisfaction of completing a task on their own.

❀

MOMS AND KIDS

In high-performance circles, professionals study the characteristics of people who reach the peak of their careers; they then strive to apply those characteristics to their own field. Suppose we studied the qualities and characteristics of great moms and dads and made strides to embody their characteristics?

Moms who are at the top of their game demonstrate incredible amounts of compassion, perseverance, and unconditional love. Whatever the reason, peak-performing moms know something we all need to know: In building a relationship with their child, they can teach and share a wisdom that at times is transmitted without words.

Peak-performing moms weave love effortlessly. We've all seen it in action. They exhibit incredible patience. They hold the highest expectations and hopes for their child, but support them forever with unconditional love no matter what they do. It's simple: Moms rule. Their handiwork will never be equaled. As we go about restoring our communities, we could learn a lot by watching moms who are good at their job.

❀ THE GAZE

"Out on the softball field was about as good as it could get," an old friend told me. "But there is something about that experience I'll never forget." Hesitating for a moment, he continued, "I'll always remember my mom sitting in the stands, rain or shine, quietly encouraging me and the whole team on. Sometimes, I think she'd be watching me instead of the game. When I think about it now, it was an incredible commitment of time, and I don't think she really cared if I hit a home run or struck out. She was there to support me."

❀ MOTHER-DAUGHTER BONDING

"My friends and I decided we really needed a way to connect with our daughters," a mom from Ohio told me. "But we wanted to do it in a creative way so it wasn't like a counseling session, so what we decided to do was form a mother-daughter book club. We all came together and selected a book to read and every week we'd discuss it. Sometimes we'd read passages out loud, reflect upon them, and then share insights and opinions."

By keeping the group small (three or four pairs of moms and daughters) and agreeing beforehand on the books they would read, this group of mothers and daughters shared some rich hours that strengthened their bonds.

"The process was so powerful," the mom said, "because by reading books together, subjects about relationships, integrity, intimacy, and sex emerged in very natural ways. I think a special bond was created not just between my daughter and me, but with the whole group. We shared our wisdom gleaned from our life experiences and our daughters responded with their incredible passion for life."

FIVE TIPS FOR HELPING OUR GIRLS

1. Talk with them about the pressures you felt when growing up and ask if they feel any of the same pressures as well.
2. Challenge and talk about the media portrayals of women, and how that makes them feel (perfect body, hair, etc.).
3. Discuss dating and sex at the appropriate time, and encourage them to stand up for themselves if they are pressured.
4. Ask if they feel safe at school, in the neighborhood, and in the community, and discuss what would make them feel safer if they don't.

> 5. Seize the opportunity to have their friends over and create the type of environment that is inviting to them.

❀

DADS AND KIDS

And what about dads? When Gwyneth Paltrow, the actress, was ten years old, her father took her to Paris. On the flight back home he asked her if she knew why he took only her. When she asked him why, he replied, "Because I wanted you to see Paris for the first time with a man who would always love you."

Unhappily, some dads aren't present in the lives of their children, but many of us see a new kind of dad emerging in our culture: a dad who changes diapers, who goes to parent-teacher conferences, and who recognizes the importance of talking and interacting with his children. We need dads who are authentic and willing to admit it when they're wrong, but who are also good at keeping the disciplinary boundaries in place. Dads are irreplaceable. Just ask moms. When moms are frustrated, they can always counter to the kids, "Wait till your dad gets home!"

❀ DAD'S CORNER

"I love coaching, but anybody can coach," said Danny Ainge, coach of the Phoenix Suns basketball team, when he quit. "But my wife has just one husband, and my children have just one father." His team was 13-7 when he quit, but he said even if the team's record "were 17-3 I'd be making the same decision."

A lot of dads would probably like to do the same thing but don't have the resources to just drop out of their work world. According to Wade Horn, president of the National Fatherhood Institute, we're living in "the best of times and the worst of times. Kids in two-parent homes have more involved fathers than past generations, but a growing number of children are deprived of fathers."

❈ DON'T IGNORE THE SIGNS

"Can your parents handle the truth?" a columnist asked teenagers. A twenty-year-old girl responded with blunt honesty: "The answer, at least in my family, is: 'Yes—but I sometimes wish they couldn't.' When I was fourteen, I told my father (a single parent) I was using drugs. His reply: 'Well, if you get all that experimentation out of your system now, you won't have a problem when you're an adult.' I wish he had flipped out and demanded that I enter treatment.

"When I lost my virginity, I told my father, and once again he handled it 'well.' My having sex didn't faze him one bit. Nor did my promiscuity throughout my teenage years. Finally, I turned myself around with no help from my 'understanding' father. I've explained to him what went wrong between us because I have younger siblings, and when they tell our father the truth, I want him not to handle it so well.

"You may think it would be great to have no rules and be able to do whatever you want. But trust me: I've been there, and it's a lonely road when nobody really cares what you do."

Our kids want us to give them constraints, boundaries, and to care about what happens to them. They want us to be outraged or upset if they go too far. Unfortunately, many parents want to be liked more than they want to challenge their kids when it's needed.

FIVE TIPS FOR HELPING OUR BOYS

1. Be sure they know it is okay to talk about and express their feelings.
2. Do something together. Boys are much more likely to open up when involved in an activity, like playing catch, fishing, or shooting hoops.
3. Acknowledge the feelings you see in boys: being afraid, disappointed, or discouraged.
4. Tell them about a letdown you experienced and how you got through it.
5. Talk with them about violence and sex in the media and how important it is for them to be responsible for their actions.

❁

PARENT WAKE-UP CALL

One mistake parents make these days is believing their kids are more mature than the parents were when they were young, and so they talk to their kids as if they were peers. As a matter of fact, kids today are not more mature than kids were twenty or thirty years ago. They are more sophisticated, but when you create a gap between sophistication and maturity, you have a generation of kids encountering situations they are unable to handle.

My two daughters and I were watching television together when a commercial came on for E.D., or "erectile dysfunction." I was desperately looking for the remote, because this wasn't a topic I really wanted to discuss. My fifteen-year-old got up and started walking toward the kitchen. "What's E.D.?" she inquired innocently. I was stunned when my thirteen-year-old said, "I know. It's impudence!"

At that moment I thanked God for not making me have to talk about it. But I also felt betrayed by television for forcing so much, so fast on our kids.

Kids today are saturated with images of sex, which appear everywhere. But they want and need to know about it, not all at once but in small doses. Parents who watch television with their kids for a single night will probably have more chances to discuss this topic than they want! But we just can't let it go undiscussed, because it starts to create a norm of behavior that anything goes and that these important topics stay in the shadows. We can start by asking questions like, "Do you think Dawson made the right decision?" "Did Ally get her information from a good source?" And we can help level the playing field by sharing with our kids: "You know, with all the emphasis on sex, you can get really confused. You're much better off waiting." We can also do something really radical—turn the TV off! But we have to remember all these issues still need to be talked about!

❀   THE BIG TALKS THAT "KINDA" HAPPEN

When I was thirteen, an announcement was made in health class that we were going to see a movie about sex the next day. The guys and I were really pumped. We thought, "It won't get much better than this." I don't think any of the guys were absent that day, but after the movie, we found that all our lofty expectations had been dashed. I, for one, was just as confused about sex as I was before! The movie was so clinical, so medical, so *not* like sex as we had imagined it!

When I arrived home that afternoon, my mom collared me and asked, "Did you understand?" I was shocked. Obviously the school had conspired with her and she knew this big day was coming. I was so embarrassed and surprised by her question that I mumbled, "Oh yeah," and that was the end of it!

From that point on I decided if I needed information I'd ask one of the older kids who lived down the block. A greaser who looked like he'd been around, he was about three years older than I; he always had a pack of cigarettes rolled up in the sleeve of his T-shirt. I couldn't depend on learning about sex from the school, and as for my mom, well, there was no precedent for us to discuss something of that nature and it seemed like both she and I were OK with things just the way they were. Ironically, after my mom read the first proof of this book, she said it was my dad who was supposed to hold the "talk," but I guess he just never got around to it!

In a survey by the Kaiser Family Foundation and Children Now released in early 1999, kids reported that they want their parents to have the "big talk" with them by the time they are thirteen. According to the study, after the age of thirteen, most youths start looking to their peers or the media for advice if their parents don't take the initiative. By engaging our kids in small discussions early, we can remove the embarrassment of talking about sex, encourage postponement of sexual activity and responsibility for it, and be there for our kids when the big questions come up.

But this also holds for discussions about drugs, peer pressure, and, believe it or not, one of the fastest-growing teen risk behaviors—gambling! Many parents are feeling so overwhelmed by these subjects that they just never get around to it. Somehow we've come to believe that there is one sacred moment when the "big talk" about one or all of these subjects has to take place, yet because it's so big, many of us can't seem to bring it up. These "big talks" are never very successful unless they have been preceded by a lot of "small talks" along the way.

❀   TIMING IS EVERYTHING

"When my daughter was twelve," a mom told me, "I was trying to decide when to have the 'talk' about sex. We had already discussed sex casually when suddenly a television program we were watching depicted it in such an overt way I knew it couldn't be overlooked. So, we talked about it a little, and a precedent had been set.

"However," she said haltingly, "one day I was jolted out of my inertia when my daughter casually said at the breakfast table, 'Mom, I don't think I'm gonna have sex for a few years.' Choking on the shredded wheat and raspberries, I tried to compose myself and replied, 'Oh really?' 'Yeah,' she said matter-of-factly. 'I don't think I'm ready.' Steadying myself, I said, 'It sounds like you've thought a lot about this.' Nodding her head, my daughter said, 'Mom, how can you not think about it? Look at the president!'

"I thought, 'If there ever was a chance, here it was.' Seizing the moment, we talked for hours. Some of the discussion was about sex. A lot of it was about being responsible and about what love was really all about. You know," this mom said with a satisfied look on her face, "I think the 'big talk' was not as hard as I expected. I think it was because we had our communication lines open and I hadn't avoided talking about it."

❀   DADS AS ENFORCERS

"One night," a dad spoke up, "my son came home with severely bloodshot eyes. When I asked him about it, my son said, 'It's no big deal; I'm just really beat,' and retired to his room. But in my 'gut,' I knew something was up. Everything told me that he had been smoking dope.

"I really didn't know how to handle it," he said. "I wanted to confront him, I wanted to stomp into his room and have it out right there. But for some reason I knew that would end in disaster. So, I summoned all my strength, knocked on his door, and entered the room. I sat down on a chair opposite my son, who was curled up on his bed. Drawing in a deep breath, I said, 'You know, we've talked about drugs, and I grew up in the drug culture, so I know what the signs are. My gut feeling tells me you've been smoking dope and that's totally unacceptable. It may seem harmless but it's not. I want you to think about it, and we'll talk about it tomorrow.' With that, I got up and left the room.

"I didn't know if I'd handled it right and I didn't know how he would respond. The next morning my son emerged from his room and after he sat down at the breakfast table he said sheepishly, 'Dad, you were right. I was smoking dope. I'm sorry. I know it was wrong, but it was so hard to say no. Marijuana is everywhere, and I just wanted to try it out and be cool.'

"I gazed at him for several moments and then said, 'You have to know how much I love you, and now how much I admire you for telling the truth." His son, who had been confronted but not shamed, nodded and said, "I love you too, Dad." Then the dad said, "You know there has to be a consequence. This may sound harsh, but I'm grounding you for a month." The dad said "I really didn't know how he'd respond, but he just nodded and said, 'Yeah, that's fair.'

"I learned a very important lesson," the dad continued. "I realized my son wanted love and approval from me just as much or maybe more than he wanted it from his peers. And I think he also wants someone to care enough to confront him. In a way," he concluded, "I think it will make it easier for him to say 'No.' After all, I told him he can tell his friends that his dad already busted him once and that he doesn't want it to happen again!"

❀   PUSHING THE ENVELOPE—KEEPING THE BOUNDARIES

"Our daughter," said an exasperated dad from Minneapolis, "our social butterfly and snowboarder, was on the phone in the kitchen while I was busy cleaning the counter. At a certain point, she put her hand over the phone and whispered, 'Dad, Abbie wants me to spend the night at her house tonight, OK?' As I considered her request, I recalled that she had spent the last two nights at a friend's house. Turning to her, I said, 'You've spent the last two nights with friends, so we need you home tonight.' The look I got at that moment registered her complete disapproval, and, not to be thwarted, she spent the next three minutes intensively lobbying to get me to see her point of view. Finally, playing her trump card, she said, 'Dad, everyone else is going to be there. It means everything to me to show up. I have to go!'

"Now, this girl is a powerful force in my universe," he continued, "and as I listened, I almost caved in. But I held my ground. As she returned to her conversation I braced myself for a 'close encounter of the third kind' that was sure to follow. So, when she hung up the phone, I waited for the fireworks. But instead of exploding, she glanced up at me and said, 'Thanks, Dad, I didn't want to go anyway!' and bounded off to her room. What I learned at that moment," he reflected, "was that it was my daughter's job to push the envelope and it was my job to keep the boundaries."

❀   ZEN PARENTING

"You know, I really have clear boundaries and expectations for my kids," said a mom as I was eavesdropping on a conversation. "They know that if they violate one of the boundaries or expectations, there is an immediate consequence." The other mom nodded and said, "I have rules in place too, but there's one other thing I always try to consider." Surprised, the first mom asked, "What's that?" As I listened, the second mom said the most remarkable thing. "Well," she started out, "first and foremost, before anything else happens, I tell them I love them and that I'm going to listen to their story." I saw mom no. 1 flinch. "What do you mean?" she asked hesitantly.

The other continued: "Even though my kids know my expectations, for me every situation is different. Each depends on what has happened in the past, and on whether they're willing to discuss it honestly with me and determine what lesson is to be learned. I have discovered that each of my kids is different and what works with one may not work with another."

I continued to eavesdrop, fascinated. This approach did not fit any parenting training courses or tips I had ever heard. I also watched the other mom squirm; her security with an immediate black-and-white consequence was shaken and her friend's approach was obviously too radical for her. Yet as I thought about this zen approach to parenting, it seemed to me that it took thought and work. Her premise revolved around keeping the relationship going; her connection with her children was of utmost importance. She was operating, I realized, on a completely different level—one at which she had to work with each situation rather than use a cookie-cutter response. Mom no. 1 was about to respond when suddenly their children appeared. As attention turned to them, I could see that mom no. 1's wheels were turning. And so were mine.

SIX IMPORTANT WAYS TO KEEP
THE BOUNDARIES

1. If your kids say, "You don't trust me," let them know you do, but that trust is earned.
2. Set curfews, stick to them, but be willing to negotiate.
3. Be aware of bleary eyes and don't let it pass if you smell alcohol or suspect use of other drugs.
4. Have little talks that will build bridges for bigger talks along the way.
5. Use teachable moments to let your kids know how you feel about sex, drugs, curfews, etc.
6. Don't ever glorify your own past drug use or talk about it in positive terms; your kids will get really confused.

❁

USING HIGH-TECH TO STAY
IN HIGH-TOUCH

Technology can be an incredible aid to keep our family connected: from e-mail to phone cards, to cell phones, these are underutilized as-sets we can use to our advantage. "We have a really active family, and with two kids in high school, it is difficult to stay in touch," a mom volunteered. "So, we gave each of our kids a cell phone so we could contact them if we needed to and so they could call us if they needed something." She continued, "You won't believe the number of times our kids have called us because they wanted to get out of a situation that they thought could lead to trouble. We even developed a system. If they wanted us to tell them they had to come home, they used the phrase 'What are you doing tonight?' We would get the cue and tell them they needed to come home immediately.

"One Friday night at about nine-thirty, I realized I couldn't remember where my daughter was supposed to be. I called her and she reminded me that she was at the local coffeehouse and that she'd be home by eleven. When she hung up, she later told me, her astonished friend looked at her dumbfounded, and said, 'Your mom really calls you up to find out where you are?' And then, gazing wistfully at her coffee, the friend said, 'I wish someone cared enough about me to want to know where I was.'"

✵ YOU'VE GOT MAIL

"E-mail has been a real godsend," a mom from Atlanta, Georgia recounted. "It's how my mom, my daughter, and I—who live in different parts of the country—stay in touch. Every day, I e-mail my mom a quick message, and when I hear back, I know everything is OK. If she doesn't respond, it means she forgot or needs help. Then I call her to check in. She really likes the security of knowing that I'm there, and it brings me peace of mind. My daughter and I don't communicate every day, but we have some conversations on e-mail that I think would have been difficult in person. It's like reviving the lost art of writing well thought out letters. It's really brought us closer in ways I never imagined."

FIVE HIGH-TECH WAYS TO KEEP
FAMILIES CONNECTED

1. Create a family Web site to which all can contribute.
2. Use e-mail to keep relatives updated on family activities and events.
3. Use the Web to research your family genealogy.
4. Make videotapes of family get-togethers and send copies to grandparents, aunts, uncles, and cousins who could not attend.
5. Enter relatives' birthdays and special days on the computer calendar.

❁

HELPING PARENTS HELPS US ALL

One afternoon, on a very full flight, I found my way toward my aisle seat. As I settled in, I noticed that in the seat next to me, looking incredibly cramped, was a mom who appeared to be really worn out as she bounced a three-year-old in her lap. After a moment or two passed, I saw her motioning to someone across the aisle who must have been her husband. It seemed it would make their trip a lot easier if I traded seats with one of them, so I offered an exchange. Within moments after moving into my new seat, another mom showed up with two children and slumped into the two seats on my side. Mom was bouncing one child on her lap and trying to read a book to the other one in the seat next to me. The next thing I knew, the two-year-old and I were busy handing the flight magazine back and forth to each other in the wonderful ritual that two-year-olds love.

When the flight attendant came by, I asked her if there were any open seats so mom could have mine for kid no. 2. The flight attendant wearily asked for my ticket. After I handed it over, she looked at it and, with an exasperated voice, said, "Sir, you're supposed to be over there" and pointed to my original seat. "Yeah, I know," I replied, "but I switched so that the other family could sit together." The flight attendant stared at me with a strange gaze. "You mean," she said, "you already gave up your seat, and you'll do it again?" I just nodded. She spun around and said she'd return in a few minutes.

Moments later she showed up with a big smile and said, "I just spoke with the gate attendant and we have found another seat for you. Follow me." I gathered up all my stuff, said good-bye to the two-year-old, and tagged along. Just before we reached the front of the plane, she turned to me with a whisper and said, "The gate attendant decided two good deeds deserve one in return. Enjoy your seat in first class." Although she was assigned to coach, she must have checked on me at least three times during the flight.

I'm not always so gracious. There are times when I just want to bury myself in a book. But I also learned a great lesson. Whenever we give to kids and families, there's always a return.

THE TOP TEN WAYS TO SAVE A KID:
IN THE FAMILY CIRCLE

1. Have high expectations for your kids, but back them with unconditional love.
2. Seize every opportunity to talk about small stuff: in the car, while watching TV, over the dinner table, before bed. (Include discussions of drugs, alcohol, and sex when appropriate and encourage your kids to defer.)
3. Within reason, check up on your teens to see if they are where they're supposed to be.
4. Get to know the parents of your kids' friends.
5. Confront your kids when necessary but don't be a snoop.
6. Show up at your kids' games, performances, and recitals (they'll be looking for you).
7. Tell your kids about their birth, and how glad you are they are in your family.
8. Remember, just because kids may dress and talk in a mature manner, they still need hugs, little talks, and lots of attention.
9. Write your kids notes reassuring them that you believe in them and love them (put them in lunch bags, under pillows, or mail them).
10. Remember what it was like being a teenager (ouch!).

FOUR

The Third Circle:
The Neighborhood

Sixty percent of American youth don't know someone well enough in their neighborhood to ask for help if they need it.

—PETER BENSON, THE SEARCH INSTITUTE

I grew up in Philadelphia in an Italian neighborhood right after World War II," a friend of mine said. "One afternoon, while at school, I mouthed off to the teacher." Chuckling, he continued, "There was no such thing as in-school suspension then and before I knew it, I was sent packing. So here I was, walking home through my Italian neighborhood, where I was met with incredulous looks by neighbors and shopkeepers and asked over and over again: 'Jimmy, what are you doing out of school?' Sheepishly, I replied, 'I got kicked out.'

"I was really surprised when they took this news personally, and everyone said something to the effect, 'Jimmy, how could you do this to us?' 'Jimmy, you represent who we are!' 'Jimmy, you are our pride and joy!' I must have received this message ten or fifteen times by the time I got home!" And then, shaking his head in wonderment, he said, "And guess who was waiting for me when I got to my doorstep? Mom! I decided then and there that nothing was worth going through this again! But I also decided," he said with a mischievous look in his eye, "that if I ever got kicked out of school again, I'd take a different route home."

Connections within our neighborhood are the building blocks of our larger communities—our kids can stand on those blocks, learn the values of that larger group, and benefit from its caring and concerned residents. In neighborhoods that are vibrant and healthy, people see, hear, and feel their neighbors' presence, their joys, and their sorrows; they respond to the group and to the individuals within it—from the toddlers to the seniors. The microcosms of our communities must be restored if our communities are to be resilient and connected places for our kids to grow up in. To revitalize our neighborhoods, we need to emerge from the cocoons of our homes, spread our wings, knock on our neighbors' door and get to know them. Once we take that small step, we can begin to reconnect the dots in our entire neighborhood, to make it safer not only for our kids, but for everyone.

REMEMBERING THE NEIGHBORHOOD

When many of us were growing up, kids in neighborhoods were connected to each other. Those who lived on the same block or in the sur-

rounding area trod the same path each day and all went to the same school. Many would stop by their friends' houses every morning on the way to school and, like snowballs rolling down a hill, would gather mass. After school and on weekends, they would congregate in the street to play lively games of kickball, pickle, jacks, jump rope, and the all-time favorite, hide 'n' seek, on a moonlit night.

Today, kids who live on the same block or in the same neighborhood often go to different schools—some of which may be a long bus ride from home. After school, kids may be home alone for hours in front of the television or the computer or on the phone until their parents arrive home from work in the evening. Teens at one end of the street may have no idea who lives at the other end. When the weekends come around, they're often off to organized activities—sports events or drama and music lessons—in different parts of the town or the city—or they're left to hang, without much to do.

By remembering the glue that connected us as kids and by reaching out to kids in our neighborhoods as adults reached out to us, we can reassemble those building blocks for our young people to stand on. This isn't rocket science. Remembering some of the ways our neighborhoods were connected when we were growing up can really help.

❀ NEIGHBORHOOD MEMORIES

"When I was a kid," a salesman said, "we had these huge neighborhood games that every kid in the neighborhood played." With that one statement, wonderful memories flooded the room as other adults recalled all the hours spent playing games with their friends. Some games were organized: hopscotch, hoops, tag football, jump rope, and Wiffle ball. Others just seemed to happen or coalesce on their own: hunting for night crawlers with flashlights and catching fireflies in a bottle topped with cheesecloth. Countless others were made up around elements in our environment: games that were played on steps or that revolved around tossing a ball off a back roof or over a house. Each game had its own rules, but the one common ingredient was incredible creativity.

One person recalled how terrified they were of the woman who would call the police the minute the football rolled onto her lawn. Others remembered broken windows, dents in parked cars, and how the police actually showed up because of a complaint. Yet we all decided it was far more valuable to have the neighborhood teeming with life rather than have all the kids inside glued to their TVs and computers. Just then, a lightbulb went on and a woman in her fifties asked the group: "Did anyone here have incredible water balloon fights?" One gentleman, almost beside himself, recalled, "I used to wait by an upstairs window and drop water balloons on kids' heads as they sprinted by!" To a person, all agreed that our neighborhoods—whether rural, suburban, or inner-city—were sanctuaries for us of incredible creativity and fun.

❈   BUYING AND SELLING COMMUNITY

Reminiscing about going door-to-door selling everything from Little League tickets to cookies to chances in the Girl Scouts raffle, one man in his fifties recounted: "We knew which houses to hit. For me, the elderly guy across the street was always good for at least three of anything, and the single guy down the block sometimes just gave us money and told us to keep whatever we had!" Another woman added, "We also knew which houses to stay away from."

And another guy laughed as he told us: "On the block where I grew up, there were some really young kids who collected a bunch of rocks and then stood out on the street corner with a hand-lettered sign that proclaimed 'Rocks for Sale.' Both my parents went out of their way to purchase some of the rocks, which made my brother and me furious. After all, if they were going to buy rocks, why didn't they buy them from us?"

Unfortunately, today, it's risky business for kids to go door-to-door in some neighborhoods without someone accompanying them, so this process for many kids no longer allows them to learn self-confidence, responsibility, and a host of other skills. However, beginning to reconnect the dots in the neighborhood can be done in small but significant ways.

❈ THAT GRANDMOTHER AT THE BUS STOP

"Each morning for the past ten years," a grandmother in a suburb of Minneapolis said, "I have stood on the street corner with the neighborhood kids while they wait to catch the bus. I check to see if they have warm hats on in winter and I ask about their homework and just how they're doing. But one day, after school, a teenage boy got mad at me and said, 'Why don't you leave us alone? What we do is none of your business!' Looking him square in the eye, I said, 'Oh, but you *are* my business!'" This simple statement summarizes the shift in our thinking that has to occur if we want to restore our neighborhoods and communities. These kids are everybody's kids. And they constantly reflect back to us the messages they have received as they move through the circles of life.

❀

CONNECTING THE
NEIGHBORHOOD DOTS

Restoring our neighborhoods means thinking in terms of connecting schools, churches, synagogues, parks and recreation centers, and businesses in taking on a neighborhood identity that we can proudly reflect to the greater community. As in all instances, it starts with one small act that can, in turn, become a point of neighborhood habit and pride.

❀ ADOPTING THE NEIGHBORHOOD KIDS

"Do you have a quarter?" a little girl asked a neighbor as she left her house in an inner-city neighborhood in Oakland, California. The woman she asked checked her purse and found she had only a $5 bill, so she offered to go to the store and buy the little girl something to eat. When the little girl was given the choice of candy or a loaf of bread and took the bread, the neighbor knew something was wrong. Not knowing the little girl, she inquired further: Did she go to school? The girl replied, "Sometimes," and then she was gone.

During the next few weeks, she kept thinking about this child. She wanted to do something, so she stopped in at the local elementary school and floored the principal by telling her she wanted to "adopt" a class all the way through college. A young boy in the class at that time says he remembers a lady who came into the classroom, gave them Christmas presents, and told them she would be a part of their lives. At monthly meetings with the class's parents and weekly meetings with the students, the principal found that often "there would be more parents at the classroom meeting than at PTA meetings for the whole school!" The principal went on to say, "I could not keep up with the ways she wanted to work with them. Tutoring, donations of encyclopedias, books, field trips . . ."

The minute she gave her commitment to see these kids through college, this "neighbor" set up trust funds, held annual fund-raisers, and became the cheerleader for the entire class. She has raised $183,000 and expects to raise another $275,000 to complete the job. In the spring of 2000 she attended numerous high school graduations, and in four more years, she'll attend ten college graduations. "When my babies walk across the stage," she said, "they can just lay me down and let me die!"

One student, who plans to become a businessman, said: "I want to own my own business and I want to help some kids like she did." Remarkably, of the twenty-three first-graders sitting in that classroom, only four didn't make it to college.

❈　　A NEIGHBORHOOD HOME AWAY FROM HOME

One day, when a friend asked a vice president of an advertising firm what she really wanted to do with her life, the executive hesitated a moment and then said she wanted to "open a home across the street from the high school in South Central Los Angeles where students could go after school to get off the dangerous streets, get a healthy snack, watch TV, and do their homework." She was startled by her response and realized she had been thinking about this for some time. The next day she quit her job, and, six months later, with only a few hundred dollars, she opened a place for kids in just three rooms in a church. The twelve kids that showed up agreed to the policy of no weapons, no drugs, and no graffiti.

After a few years a new facility has many sponsors and a 10,000-square-foot building; more than three hundred young people—hard-core gang members to straight-A students from the ages of nine to twenty—come "home" every day. The facility has its own school, library, computer lab, and recording studio. The kids can participate in yoga, dance, kick boxing, and poetry classes.

The former vice president says: "Our goal is to reclaim the children from the streets and make the neighborhood safe. It's a big job. Can one person make a difference? In spite of obstacles, shortcomings and impossible odds, I say absolutely!"

FIVE EASY WAYS YOU CAN CREATE A KID-FRIENDLY NEIGHBORHOOD

1. Agree to abide by neighborhood speed limits and post "Slow" signs.
2. Buy whatever kids who come to your door are selling.
3. Put up an adjustable basketball hoop so kids and adults can gather, shoot hoops, and have fun.
4. Take your kids with you when you help out a senior (shovel a walk, buy groceries).
5. Set out a bench on your front porch and engage kids who pass by to visit with you.

❀ SMALL STEPS WITH STREET KIDS

Used to working with street kids living on the edge in a neighborhood by a large university, a deacon at an Episcopal church said, "I thought I had gotten used to these kids dying horrible deaths. I had been doing this work for some time. But when one boy, whom I had come to truly love, overdosed, I was so heartbroken I said to myself, 'I don't think he would have died if he had for one time in his life just been adored.'"

Resolving to create a place where kids could come without the fear of being judged, or hassled, or frisked, she opened the Arts Center for Street Kids in Seattle. There they can choose to create a tie-dyed T-shirt or work with clay, paint, paper, beads, and macramé. Most of all, she says, "we wanted to create a sacred space, where it was quiet and the kids wouldn't have to think about their next fix or the cops." There are expectations for all the kids who come. They have to follow the rules: no drugs, no weapons, no illegal substances or activities, and respect must be shown to all.

Reflecting on their lives, she says, "Most of these kids are really brave. They have left very dangerous and abusive homes—some where parents used drugs or abused them constantly—and they have chosen to live in a different way. It's a miracle they haven't taken their lives. They've chosen life over death. What they learn at the Arts Center is basic stuff, like systematic thinking, delayed gratification (waiting for your paint to dry), how to give and receive, and, hopefully, one day, how to ask for help from social services on how to get your life back together."

She concludes, "Many of the kids have no sense of self-worth. They have been used all of their lives. The Arts Center allows them to sit in the lap of God's love from one to five P.M. two times a week."

❁ PROM NIGHT FOR PROMISING KIDS

At a downtown alternative school for homeless kids in a large urban area, something magical happened. These kids, who have experienced nightmarish lives—from parental abuse, pregnancies, and addiction to poverty and hunger—had a chance to be "kids again." With donations of black socks from the police department, beauty sessions from a local hair salon, dresses, shoes, and jewelry from a national secretaries organization, and limos from a limo company, as well as corsages and boutonnieres from a local florist and a photographer who took pictures for free, community members supported their young people with their hearts and pocketbooks. "This event is amazing," said one homeless girl. "It makes me feel very grateful." "They got to enter the fantasy world of their prom," said one of the social workers, "for one magical night." We, as neighbors and a country, are only as great as we treat our most disenfranchised people. In this case, we can all be very proud.

❁

LIVING IN COCOONS

Remember when neighbors washed their cars in front of their houses and talked to each other over backyard fences as they mowed and watered their lawns? Kids and their parents would look out for the el-

derly couple across the street. People not only knew each other, they knew who was ill, who had slipped on the ice, who was about to get married, and who was going on a vacation. Those in the field of research might call all these activities "promising practices." Most of us would call them "no-brainers."

But today, with the aid of a garage-door opener, we can get to and from work without ever having to make any connection whatsoever with anyone else on the block. The only time many of us run into our neighbors is when we are putting out the garbage in our robes—hoping we won't be seen. Technology, in the form of television, VCRs, computers, and the Internet, has cocooned us in our homes. We may be connected globally, but the local ties have been severed.

When I ask community members who grew up twenty or thirty years ago where they went if they needed a couple of eggs or a cup of sugar, the overwhelming response is "Next door!" Today, the overwhelming response is "To the store!"

❀   AMBASSADORS NEXT DOOR

In a small New England community, an "Adopt a Neighborhood" initiative is alive and well. The program encourages two or more families to adopt their street and become their neighborhood's ambassadors. These ambassadors share information with their neighbors about ways to build a healthy neighborhood for families and kids, and they hope that through this effort, neighbors will become more connected, watch out for each other's kids, and maybe even create neighborhood service projects. Neighbors are starting to take personal responsibility for what goes on, to consciously reach out to each other, and to be comfortable enough to ask for help or even a couple of eggs. "We want to help return power to people at a local level," the community coordinator says. "It's really bringing people and kids together in a very grassroots way."

❁ STUDYING THE NEIGHBORHOOD

"Do you know your neighbors?" "Do you know how many kids live on the block?" were just a few of the questions that were part of a neighborhood survey done by college students in a neighborhood renewal project in suburban Minneapolis. As the students collected the data, along with the help of residents, they created a neighborhood map and a phone tree so everyone could keep in touch. Next, they held a neighborhood meeting to begin to build relationships, discuss common ground, and agree on boundaries for the kids. Finally they decided to hold a parade. Parents, seniors, singles, and kids marched around the neighborhood holding balloons, pushing strollers, and getting to know each other.

❁ THE FRONT-PORCH INITIATIVE

"Eating cookies and talking," a member of an Ohio initiative group told me, "is now the order of the day in our neighborhood. Many of us grew up on streets where homes had large front porches where we could congregate and chat. They were even great seats to watch a touch football or pickup baseball game. But," he said, shaking his head, "the backyard has become a hiding place and refuge for families. Maybe it's time to come out of hiding." Then, becoming more animated, he continued, "Neighbors are encouraged to sit on their front porches in the evening with a plateful of cookies and to invite passersby for a cookie and some conversation. Some of the kids just come by for the cookies, but with each visit we learn a little more about them. It sounds so simple," he related, "but our neighborhood does feel safer. After all, now we know most everyone who lives on the block, and we also know who serves our favorite cookies!"

❀ DISCONNECTED "HOODS"

"Our neighborhood had changed a lot over the years," an older gentleman said, "but I told myself I was going to become a one-man welcoming committee and turn things around. I saw a moving van down the block and I figured this is where I could begin. I walked up to the young guy standing near the van, stuck out my hand and said, 'Welcome to the neighborhood.' The man looked back at me, surprised, and, taking my hand, he replied, 'Thanks for the greeting, but I've lived here for the past five years, and we're moving this weekend.'"

❀
NEIGHBORLY WAYS

Reconnecting our neighborhoods will happen when we get inspired and regain the habits of a good neighborhood. One resident of a cul-de-sac neighborhood told me that on nice spring weekends all the residents unroll their hoses, bring out buckets and sponges, and work together to clean the aluminum siding of all their houses, one at a time. The neighborhood sparkles with a sense of comradeship and cleanli-

ness. One day, the resident told a colleague at work how all his neigh-bors help each other out. His fellow employee looked at him, befuddled, and said with all sincerity, "What are you, Amish or something?"

Most of us yearn for the sense of community and belonging that those neighbors have. Sometimes the vision we have is idealized and sometimes it's actualized. The movie Witness *includes two remarkable scenes of "connectedness" as a way of life. The first is a barn raising. Everyone in the neighborhood shows up to help build a barn; walls are built, tools are shared, skills are learned, and the profound satisfaction of watching a barn being built in a day is felt by all. During the fever-ish activity, the smells of a fabulous meal being prepared promises a great reward. Young and old alike are actively engaged in the process that is a service to a neighbor. There is cooperation, competition, and collaboration, but more than anything else, the activity is natural. It is a practice that is part of the Amish culture and a way of life. In the sec-ond scene, neighbors respond to the ringing of a bell that signals a need for help, and by their presence alone, they resolve the final crisis.*

Although few of us know how to raise a barn (or live near some-one who needs one), there are many aspects of our neighborhoods that need rebuilding and repair. We can look around us, make a plan, lift a telephone, call a meeting, and get neighbors and our kids involved in the "raising" of our neighborhoods.

❀ CULTIVATING CARING NEIGHBORHOODS

"My mother wouldn't let us associate with kids who were get-ting in trouble," a young man who lived in an inner-city neighbor-hood said. "She told us to keep to ourselves and find constructive activities. I hated it then, but now I'm glad."

Today, this young man sits on a neighborhood renewal council, and he's part of the solution. The neighborhood council has created opportunities for kids to work with adults to fix up houses, tutor younger students, and help the elderly. Recently, young people cleaned up a donated, vacant house adjacent to a neighborhood park and are working to change it into a youth center. The project's site coordinator applauds the involvement of the youth in neighborhood renewal and says, "These kids are bright and ambitious. They are determined to create change and bring pride back to their neighborhoods. I believe they are going to do it too!"

Our kids, when invited into the process, whether it's serving on a neighborhood board or a YMCA advisory council, want to give back when they can. Like adults, some will come to one meeting and never show again, and others (sometimes the ones we least expect) will come ready to work with their sleeves already rolled up. They clearly understand what needs to be done, and, when they're not marginalized and left out, will multiply all our efforts.

❀   CRAZY RUTH

Much to the horror of her friends, a grandmother who lived in a gang-infested neighborhood would go out for a walk alone every day. "Ruth," they'd say to her, "are you crazy? You're gonna get mugged!" But Ruth had a unique strategy. Rather than avoid the kids, she'd engage them. She'd approach them, ask their names, tell them stories about the neighborhood and about their parents, grandparents, and aunts and uncles. And she'd share candy with them. As it turned out, Ruth had the freedom to walk wherever she pleased. The word was out that you didn't mess with Ruth. Some said she was protected. Ruth said it was love. "All these kids really want is to be recognized and respected," she volunteered. In her grandmotherly wisdom, she also observed, "A gang provides them what they haven't got from their family or community. I try to give them some of these essentials whenever I can."

Ruth, in her no-nonsense and courageous approach, invited kids into her circle. These kids, like everyone else, were really looking for love.

❀   NEIGHBORHOOD POLICING

As two officers patrolled an inner-city neighborhood in Newark, New Jersey, on foot, they came upon a pregnant woman with a young child at a bus stop being harassed by a drunk man. Both the woman and child were obviously terrified. The officers, who had gone to great lengths to get to know the residents of the neighborhood, knew the man and addressed him by name: "Joe, you must leave this woman alone." When Joe protested, one of the officers took him firmly by the shoulders, turned him around, and began walking him away from the woman. Joe continued to protest: "I'm not doing anything wrong." His street companions, who were standing alongside nearby buildings and watching, began to comment: "Oh, oh, Joe wants to get arrested."

The officer walked Joe about ten yards away from the woman and instructed him: "I'm going to let you go, but keep walking. I don't want you to bother this woman anymore." Joe continued to protest, and when the officer let him go, he took a couple of steps forward, then tried to run around the officers and back to the woman and child. The officers immediately grabbed Joe, wrestled him to the ground, handcuffed him, and called for a car to take him to the station for booking.

During the twenty-minute wait for the car, Joe continued to

protest, ranting and raving in a drunken fashion. One officer held Joe down, while the other exchanged comments with citizens, including the woman and child. Joe's street colleagues never came to his aid and ridiculed him for his behavior. Finally, a police car came, the officer put Joe in the backseat, the car pulled away, and the citizens dispersed. The power of building relationships and knowing the names of the residents in the neighborhood saved the day.

QUICK NEIGHBORHOOD QUIZ

YES	NO	
☐	☐	My kids know someone well enough in our neighborhood to ask for help in time of emergency (ask your kids).
☐	☐	I know the kids in my neighborhood well enough to offer help in an emergency.
☐	☐	I know the names of most of the kids in my neighborhood.
☐	☐	I say hello to kids who live on our block.
☐	☐	If a kid comes to my door selling something, I buy.
☐	☐	Kids feel safe in our neighborhood (ask them).
☐	☐	I go out of my way to stop at every lemonade stand.

✸ PAINTING A WELCOME SIGN

"My sister and her husband were going to paint their newly purchased home," a woman said with a smile. "But we had something else planned." On the day this was to happen, suddenly and quite unexpectedly the yard was filled with friends from their church and people from their new neighborhood who were ready to do the job. This was a no-nonsense group. The windows were taped and the siding was scraped in no time. Even kids were shown how to paint and were given jobs that matched their abilities. The whole project was completed by the afternoon. When it was done, everyone sat down and shared a meal to which all had contributed. "My sister was so overcome by the support that she broke into tears."

Celebrating a move and being welcomed into a neighborhood is an important ritual. In the movie *It's a Wonderful Life,* a neighborly celebration is held when an Italian family buys its first home. Bread and wine are shared as symbols of good fortune and a happy household. For some, a prayer or a blessing is appropriate.

We can start to revive this ritual by just showing up at a new neighbor's door with cookies and a few kind words. From that one small act, wonderful relationships can grow.

FIVE WAYS TO WELCOME NEW NEIGHBORS

1. Hold a block party or picnic to welcome and meet the newcomers. Have games planned so kids and adults can get to know each other.
2. Invite a new family on a walk of the neighborhood.
3. Offer to take the new neighbors' children to the movies while Mom and Dad unpack.
4. Present new neighbors with flower seeds or bulbs to recognize this new beginning in their lives.
5. Give them a short list of baby-sitters, nearby parks, and recreation services for kids.

CREATING A CARING, CONNECTED NEIGHBORHOOD FOR OUR KIDS

WHAT DOES IT LOOK LIKE?

- Neighbors waving to each other
- Parents keeping an eye on their kids and on others
- Kids playing in yards and on the street
- Lemonade stands and hopscotch squares
- Neighbors chatting on porches, in yards, across fences, or on the sidewalk

- Retailers displaying kids' artwork
- Spaces for community members to congregate and chat
- Kids delivering papers, shoveling snow, and picking up trash
- All the neighbors having a block party or a garage sale

WHAT DOES IT SOUND LIKE?

- Children laughing
- Adults and kids saying hi to each other
- Games being played on the street or sidewalks
- Neighbors calling kids by their names
- Telephones ringing as neighbors call those who are housebound
- Local television and radio stations broadcasting supportive messages about kids and their achievements
- Community members speaking proudly of their youth

WHAT DOES IT FEEL LIKE?

- An inviting place
- Somewhere anyone would *want* to live
- Warm, connected
- Caring, loving
- Supportive
- Safe for kids and everyone

THE TEN TOP WAYS TO SAVE A KID:
IN THE NEIGHBORHOOD CIRCLE

1. Learn the names of all the kids on your block.
2. Invite a neighbor with kids for dinner.
3. Have "safe houses" clearly marked where kids can go if they need help.
4. Hold gatherings of adults and kids throughout the year—picnics, barbecues, winter walks, pumpkin carvings, game days.
5. Create spaces in your neighborhood where adults and children can gather—benches near a basketball hoop, for example.
6. Remember, the sounds of skateboarding means kids are doing something constructive (getting exercise and not getting into trouble).
7. Put up traffic signs: "Drive slowly! We love our kids."
8. Get the kids on your block involved in drawing up a neighborhood map and creating a phone tree network.
9. Adopt a "senior citizen" on the block and watch out for him or her. (Kids can shovel walks, rake leaves, etc.)
10. Take a walk through your neighborhood on a regular basis; admire the flowers, get to know the dogs, and acknowledge the kids.

FIVE

The Fourth Circle:
The Community

A man of true courage leaves
No child unguarded.
He knows that way
Lies eternity.

—LAO-TZU

In some remote African villages," shared a woman with our group, "when the father becomes aware that his wife is pregnant, he starts building a birthing hut. It is believed that the more elaborate the hut, the greater his love and support is for his partner. When the birth is imminent, a group of wise women gather around to nurture the wife through this experience. Villagers bring flowers and food to show their connection and ongoing support, and as the labor intensifies, the villagers sing and play music that reflects the phases of the birth. During the last phases of labor, the music grows stronger and stronger, and when the birth of the child is announced, the entire village celebrates!" The arrival of a newborn to our community is one of life's greatest miracles. And how we see and honor this valuable resource as it "grows" in our community will predict our very future.

From the moment our kids are born, they will begin to encounter a spectrum of experiences waiting for them in our communities. From interactions with teachers, coaches, ministers, and a powerful array of adults, the quality of all their experiences will help shape whom they will become. I often ask audiences across the country, "When a young person turns eighteen, what are the characteristics or qualities that you want them to have learned or gained after walking through the many different experiences your community offers?" The answers are consistent: responsibility, a sense of self-worth, a desire to give back to the community, and respect for self and others. When I ask the million-dollar question, "Whose responsibility is it to see that this happens?" the response is always, "First the family—and then everyone!" At this moment, an AHA! experience occurs. It becomes apparent that we are all responsible for the kids in our community because we are creating the mirrors of experience that they will reflect back to us. Our kids are a very important barometer of how we are all doing, and if they are in crisis, we as a culture and community are in crisis as well. We begin to change the climate of the circle of community as we begin to acknowledge their presence, draw on their unique gifts and skills, and provide them with an opportunity to contribute and make a difference. When we do this, we actually gain an increment of our own lost power—power that will bubble up in sometimes the most unexpected ways. For, rather than waiting for somebody else to do it, or for a program to "fix" our kids, we realize that ordinary adults and kids, together, can do extraordinary things.

❀

TENDING A GARDEN— CARING FOR TEENS

One of the most powerful things we can do at the community level is to extend invitations to our kids to participate in community life. In agrarian cultures kids were needed to help bring in the crops, and if they didn't work, quite often the family didn't eat. Most kids, if given the choice, would rather participate in meaningful ways in their community rather than hang out at the mall. Our great challenge is to include our kids—beginning when they are very young, so they feel valued, affirmed, and connected to their community.

❀ PLANTING AND HARVESTING

Community members in Roswell, New Mexico, were compiling a list of outstanding resources that were already in place for kids there: Boys' and Girls' Clubs, youth sports, the YMCA, the community theater. When a middle-aged woman raised her hand and said, "I have an acre of gardens in my backyard. I have always had a dream that the children and the adults in our community could come and garden together. When you garden, something magical happens. You connect with the earth. You talk about things that run deep. And you build something together that lasts a lifetime."

When she finished, the whole group was quiet. It sounded so simple, so real. When youth and adults work side by side, there is such an incredible opportunity for all the good stuff to happen—

building strong relationships, seeing the fruits of our labor, and taking pride in an accomplishment. And as I basked in her suggestion, I thought of the movie *The Karate Kid,* in which the karate teacher, Mr. Miyagi, begins to mentor his teenage student "Daniel-san" by showing him the fine art of trimming a bonsai tree. The relationship that grows between them is that of mentor and child—one that grows symbolically from the plant's roots.

❀ NURTURING OUR RESOURCE

"You know," a community mobilizer said from a rugged, popular Idaho ski community, "kids between the ages of fifteen and twenty-one are between worlds. For a lot of them there isn't anything to do, so they end up in trouble. They end up drinking out in the woods or trying to get into bars. They need another option." After sharing this with some community members, several responded by saying, "C'mon, these kids can't be bored. They have a ski mountain. It's one of the best in the world!" Feeling like a broken record, she sighed and responded, "But you forget, skiing is possible only part of the year, and for many of our local kids, it's too pricey—and, by the way, the highest-risk hours when kids get in the most trouble are right after school!

"I guess," she continued, "that being a broken record does pay off! We now have a coffee shop for teens, which provides them with a place to go at night and we're currently setting up after-school homework and mentoring programs." Laughing, she insightfully concluded, "We put a lot of resources into environmental issues in our area. My goal is to make sure our kids are at least as important as salmon!"

FIVE EFFECTIVE WAYS TO NURTURE YOUR COMMUNITY'S TEENS

1. Create youth advisory boards for new projects.
2. Hold a "Listening to Youth" night and have kids talk about what it is like to live in your community.
3. Think about mentoring: How can youth take on roles and work with adults who will teach them responsibility?
4. Ask "Where's our youth?" at every meeting.
5. Team up youth with local service clubs.

❁

IN OUR SCHOOLS

Because our children spend a great deal of time during their formative years in schools, teachers and administrators can have an enormous impact. Many of our educators are fiercely committed to our children and are determined to make a difference in their lives. Yet, schools are continually asked to do more and more. Principals and superintendents that I encounter across the country tell me they are putting in seventy-hour weeks. Nevertheless, teachers and administrators are often blamed for things that are out of their control. As one superintendent said to me: "Have you ever noticed we don't have a drug problem in our community during the summer?" When I related this story to a group of principals, one of them raised his hand and said, "Yeah, and the same thing is true about lice!"

There are so many caring educators, but with class sizes so large and personal contact minimized, many kids are falling through the cracks. We need to come up with strategies that create more connected, caring school climates. Through their caring and creative ways, those who work with our kids in schools play an instrumental role in the fourth circle. As one teacher told me: "I've taught for twenty years and I've finally learned what my true role is in the classroom. It's my job to identify my students' strengths and reflect them back to them continuously."

❀   FROM BREAKING TO TAKING RESPONSIBILITY

"Over a period of time," a long-term substitute music teacher at a junior high told me, "I discovered that several violins had been broken by being smashed against the wall in the music room. I thought I knew who did it, but I couldn't catch him in the act. One day, spontaneously, I asked the boy I suspected of the vandalism if he would be responsible for the key to the instrument room. Noticing the look of shock on his face, I asked him to be sure students could get in the room to get their instruments and to put them away. For the next few days," she said, shaking her head, "I thought I had made a terrible mistake and I had visions of all the instruments mutilated! But the most remarkable thing happened. Not only were there no more broken instruments, but the boy began polishing and organizing every instrument in the room!"

NORTH CHICAGO
PUBLIC LIBRARY

❈ MR. HOLLAND'S REPRIEVE

In the wonderful movie *Mr. Holland's Opus,* Glenn Holland, played by Richard Dreyfuss, is a high school music teacher who changes kids' lives using the vehicle of music. However, in the end, his music program is slashed when the school decides to get back to the "basics," which doesn't include music.

Unfortunately, this scenario is being repeated again and again. Sports programs and computer labs are being lavishly funded, while the arts go begging. Richard Toure, senior editor of *Connect for Kids,* reports that "new research reveals what many in arts education have known for years." UCLA Department of Education studies revealed in 1997 that students in the eighth and tenth grades who were very involved with the arts in and out of school consistently had higher standardized test scores and were less likely to drop out than kids who were not involved with the arts, and that kids who are involved in organized music programs have the lowest substance-abuse rates of all kids in their age group. There is an old Chinese saying that we might do well to take to heart. It is, "Education should begin with poetry, be strengthened by character, and consummated with music."

❈ CATCHING KIDS DOING SOMETHING RIGHT

With a cellular phone strapped to her side, a middle school principal began cruising the halls with a mission. Seeing a seventh-grader reach over and pick up a piece of trash and toss it in the garbage, she decided to seize the moment. Going up to the boy, she said, "Josh, could I speak with you for a moment?" You can guess what Josh's first thought was! "Josh," she said, "by picking up that paper and tossing it, it shows you really care about our school! Keep it up!"

Then the principal whipped out her phone and said, "Josh, is there anybody we could call up right now and tell what a great kid you are?" Josh, who was a sharp kid, replied, "Could we do a conference call?" After a good chuckle, they decided to call Josh's stepmom. When Mom answered the phone, the principal said, "Hello, Mrs. Turner. This is the principal at your son's school." What do you think Mom's first response was? She started backpedaling rapidly: "Well, Josh is from a first marriage—"

"Mrs. Turner," the principal said in a heartfelt manner, "I'm not calling because anything's wrong. I just caught Josh doing something wonderful at our school and I wanted to tell you what a great kid he is and how much we enjoy having him here." Handing the phone to Josh, the principal said, "Josh, would you like to say a few words to your mom?" Josh took the phone and swelled with pride, and said, "Yo, Mom!"

Capitalizing upon the resources we have at present, and adding a dose of creativity, we can change the culture with something as simple as a phone call!

❀ TEST SCORES GOING UP

"Because we want to get test scores up," a principal in Arlington, Texas, told me, "I asked several teachers to tutor certain students during the year. After all," the principal said, "we're judged by our scores and I was looking for any edge." A few weeks after the test, the principal was elated. The test scores for the school were a dramatic improvement over the prior year, and, with the scores in hand, the principal personally went around thanking the teachers who had volunteered to tutor these kids. Chuckling, he told me "I was dumbfounded at their response. All of the teachers said, somewhat embarrassed, 'I don't want to admit it, but I didn't have time to tutor the students I said I would. But every day I did go out of my way to say hi and to see how they were doing!'"

Feeling valued, loved, and acknowledged may have a direct connection to everyone's production and test scores. Knowing someone cares about you in any environment has direct and obvious benefits.

❀ COUNTERING CLIQUES

In the aftermath of the recent horrible school shootings, many schools across the country are convening focus groups of students to discuss the importance of connecting with everyone at the school and not stereotyping kids due to the way they look or dress. One student from Denver told me how he and his friends used to sit at the "cool" lunch table and how they wouldn't allow anyone else to sit there. "Now I look back, and I can see I was a jerk." One junior told the middle school students that a lot of the kids that didn't seem to fit in at that age turned out to be the nicest kids by high school. "Getting this clique thing worked out in seventh and eighth grade," another senior concluded, "will make high school the best time of your life."

Some middle and high schools are trying to change this situation by holding Accomplishment Assemblies, which are designed to honor the accomplishments of all kids, not just a few. There are awards for actors, stage producers, snowboarders, youth entrepreneurs, debaters, and those who serve the community and the school, as well as for those who do well in athletics and academics. Letterman jackets are given to those who participate in a range of activities, and not just sports. In these Accomplishment Assemblies, schools recognize that intelligence and talent come in many packages and that no one contribution is better than another.

❀   LOOKING FOR ATTENTION

Having been recently trained in a new discipline strategy, a teacher said: "If a young person acted out, I was supposed to write his or her name on the board and not say a word. If they continued any inappropriate behavior I was supposed to put a check after their name. Students who accumulated three checks would have to stay after school."

About two weeks after she instituted this discipline strategy, "a really strange thing happened," she said. "One boy, who had been well behaved all day, started acting up during the final hour of school. He accumulated checks so quickly and so often that he had to stay after school almost every day. I was concerned about his change in behavior so I asked my colleagues if they knew of a reason for this new behavior, but no one did. Finally, after seven consecutive days of having to keep the boy after school, I suddenly realized what was motivating him. I realized that he wanted to stay after school and have some undivided attention!

"Pulling him aside at lunch, I said to him, 'You know what? If you want to stay after school, you can do it without getting checks on the board. I enjoy having you there and would really like your help with a few things.' Looking as though the weight of the world had just been lifted off his back, he smiled and said, 'Really?' From that day on he showed up after class almost every day—sometimes to help clean up, sometimes to talk, or sometimes just to hang out and do his homework."

FIVE GREAT WAYS TO CREATE CARING SCHOOLS

1. Create a council of students representing each clique and discuss how each can be recognized and valued.
2. Invite parent volunteers, local police and firemen, and college students to help on the playground. Invite artists to work in the hallways during school.
3. Create homework clubs after school and invite high school students, retired teachers, and college students to act as tutors.
4. Use recess as a time to teach inclusion (play games; stress getting along; include everyone).
5. Create focus groups of kids, community members, and faculty members, and have all describe—and work to create—the kind of school climate they want.

IN OUR CHURCHES, SYNAGOGUES, AND TEMPLES

For some kids, participation in religious services and affiliated activities seems natural and comfortable. Some attend because they want to, and others go because they're forced to. But as kids get older, they are like adults: they "vote with their feet." If they aren't getting something out of it, they'll have a million creative excuses for why they can't or won't attend religious services or religious school.

I remember church as a rather mysterious place. I knew that something magical was supposed to happen. After all, there were all these incredible statues, rituals, and prayers that seemed very old and very important. But I was never sure what they meant to me. In high school, I went to church so I could play on the church basketball team—now, that was a motivator. You had to attend church twice a month to be eligible, and to this day I remember some of my teammates and I would walk over to our best basketball player's house and drag him out of bed to church. He was our star center and we couldn't afford to lose him.

Today, as I talk with church youth workers, I find they are really motivated but also really frustrated. Parents drop kids off in front of the church or synagogue or temple and show up an hour and a half later to pick them up. Many of those kids are disengaged and many of the youth workers are at a loss. "What do we do?" they ask. One of the first ways is to involve our kids and their parents in ways that translate spirituality and service into meaningful actions in their lives.

FAMILY SUNDAY SCHOOL

Each weekend morning across America the same scene is reenacted again and again. Parents roll up in front of their church or synagogue, drop off their kids, try not to make eye contact with anyone for fear of embarrassment, and return a bit later to pick the kids up. Another variation on this theme is that, after the service, adults sip coffee and munch on donuts while their kids sit in a classroom "getting religion." As an astute observer put it, "Most religious education programs are like the food in my refrigerator: not quite good enough to eat, but not quite bad enough to throw out."

What if religious education involved the whole family? Suppose the kids and adults weren't segregated but integrated, to talk about their faith, and to learn and teach spiritual lessons to others? Out of this approach, powerful intergenerational relationships are built: a five-year-old and a fifty-year-old could read religious texts about kindness, or a small group of young and old in the congregation might act out a lesson in compassion, and all engage in music, art, and drama. The same intergenerational groupings could take their faith into the community and do local service projects together to really walk the faith.

Just as our spiritual life shouldn't be separate from our everyday life, we shouldn't separate our generations when putting our faith into action.

MUSING OF A MENTOR

"A young man approached me one day after worship service," an older Congregational Church member said. "I knew him casually as one of the kids who attended church with his family. 'Mr. Stewart,' he began, 'would you be my mentor?' 'Gosh, I don't know. What's involved?' I replied. 'Well, you're supposed to be sort of a spiritual friend to me during my confirmation.' 'How long will that take?' I inquired. 'Three years,' the boy replied. 'That's a long time,' I responded, chuckling. 'I don't know whether I'll be around,' I said, pointing out that I was eighty. 'At the rate you're going, I think you'll make it,' he said, smiling. 'Might be OK,' I mused. 'Let me think it over, and I'll call you,' I replied, departing with his 'Thank you' ringing in my ears.

"On the way home, my wife and I discussed his request. 'You should be honored,' she said. 'You've always enjoyed teaching Sunday school. Why not give it a try?' So I accepted his invitation. I've enjoyed a fine experience, one well-expressed in this bit of philosophy Shane later sent me: 'Some people come into our lives and quietly go. Others stay for a while and leave footprints on our hearts, and we are never the same.'

"It took about a year for us to find a comfortable relationship. My awkward questions and his 'Yep' and 'Nope' answers did not move the process rapidly. I didn't want to invade his lifestyle too much, and he wasn't sure just what this old geezer was like. But we worked at it, chatted about odds and ends when we met, and exchanged greeting cards at appropriate times. I took pictures of his confirmation class and of soccer games he refereed. I began seeing his name in the local paper on school honor-role lists and in the church bulletin as an acolyte or usher. I put these articles and others into a scrapbook, which we presented to him at his confirmation.

"We are still going strong seven years since he asked me to be his mentor. He stops by once in a while for a soda and cookies, sometimes with his girlfriend. Last fall he went off to college. 'We'll still be good friends,' he assures me. But my wife and I miss him, just like when our kids left the nest. So long, good buddy."

❁ NAMING AND CLAIMING OUR KIDS

"We wanted to make our synagogue more open and friendly," a member said. "So, our board decided we should issue name tags to everyone as they came through the door. After several weeks, we really noticed a difference and were busy patting ourselves on the back. People were much more freely interacting—it was magic, knowing someone's name. But one day we realized something was terribly amiss. We had a whole group of no-names! We had left out the kids. Rectifying this oversight as fast as we could, more magic started happening. The kids suddenly took on identities, and adults started making connections and saying, 'Oh, you're Seth! And Joe and Melissa are your parents! Now I know who they've been talking about!' It was like these kids were now real persons and not anonymous fireballs of energy. They were named and claimed! Now, introductions have become a whole lot easier, and one of the goals at coffee hour is to teach our 'newfound kids' how to introduce and greet someone by name!"

FIVE EASY WAYS TO KEEP FAITH WITH KIDS

1. Make name tags for everyone (including kids) in your church or synagogue to promote relationships and friendship.

2. Involve kids in intergenerational service projects and talk about issues of faith and life with them.

3. Invite teens to help teach religious classes and train them to deliver sermons during services.

4. Hold intergenerational spiritual activities where one virtue is identified and discussed each month.

5. Create a youth advisory group to suggest positive ways to involve kids of all ages.

ON THE SPORTS FIELD

Americans seem to be obsessed with sports, with winning, and with being number one. Almost as soon as kids are out of their toddler years, they are engaged in some sport—some are into several sports by the time they are in the third or fourth grade. Our culture's obsession with athletics and with winning leads to intense competition at very early ages.

As a result, our kids often lose sight of the real reasons for playing team sports: the joys of physical activity, learning new skills, playing with others, building relationships and learning sportsmanship. Many of the kids who may not be athletically gifted but who want to play end up sitting on the bench or never trying out in the first place, because in order to win, a coach always has to play the very best play-

ers. This approach feeds the stratification that begins in elementary schools, intensifies in middle schools, and reaches outrageous proportions in high schools. The "jocks" are elevated to vastly superior positions in the school hierarchy because the value placed upon their talents is so high.

When I turned out for football at my high school after playing for years in the junior leagues, I was in for a big surprise. Sixty guys showed up for practice! I was patiently waiting my turn in line to get a uniform when the sophomore football coach walked up to me and stunned me by asking, "How tall is your dad?" Mumbling, I said, "Five feet eleven inches." Nodding, he pointed to another line. About five minutes later I realized I wasn't going to get a uniform! "Wait a minute," I screamed inside. "Talk to my junior league coaches or somebody. I at least deserve a chance to try out." I returned home in tears. And in that moment I realized how powerful coaches are. They hold many keys to building self-confidence in all our kids.

How do we deal with these very real issues in our kids' lives? A high school in Montana has a "no cut" policy in sports. In other words, kids who turn out make the team! Maybe they don't play all the time, but they all have a chance to participate, to build relationships, and to be a part of something bigger than themselves. In many middle schools across the country, the cheerleading squads consist of fifty or sixty kids. Those who have the desire and show up are on the squad. What a great way to build self-worth and healthy kids!

America's obsession with being number one or always first is a little scary. If you are at a sports event or watching a game on television during which the camera pans the crowd or the team, you might see fans and players (even if the team is in last place or losing the game) screaming, "We're number one!" I often want to say to them: "No, you're number four, but that's OK!" In America, we have turned win-

ning into the only thing. Although sports develop an array of positive characteristics in our kids, it also has given birth to acts of violence and the illusion that the only acceptable place to be is first.

✸ I LIKE MIKE

One year I was watching the NCAA Men's Championship basketball game, but, being from the West Coast, I didn't really have a team to root for. Duke, the perennial power and lopsided favorite, was playing Connecticut. I decided to go with the underdog because Duke, I figured, was a basketball factory that pumped players into the big leagues. The game was really close throughout, and Duke, trailing with but a few seconds left, threw up a desperation shot that fell short. Mighty Duke had fallen.

As I watched the interviews with the coaches that followed the game, I was startled by the response of Duke coach Mike Krzyzewski, who was asked how he felt when his top-rated team lost the national championship. Without hesitating, he said how proud he was of his players and concluded with the astounding statement: "I don't coach for winning, I coach for relationships." I thought that for a coach at that level of competition to make that statement was profound. Now, none of my kids are going to college on a basketball scholarship, but if they did, Duke would be at the top of my list.

✸ CRAZED PARENTS

"Our baseball league was really struggling," a community member from Northfield, Minnesota, said. "It wasn't the kids who were the problem, it was the parents! We were having difficulty getting anyone to umpire or coach because the parents were so verbally abusive to the 'umps,' and oftentimes toward the other team. We held a board meeting," he continued, "and came up with an idea. We created a card that we would give to parents who were being obnoxious. The card read something to the effect, 'We enjoy having you here, but unless you cool it, we're going to stop the game until you leave.'" Laughing, he said, "We've only given out a few cards because the word circulated like wildfire amongst the parents. Now, we have an abundance of umpires, happier coaches, and kids who can just be kids and play the game."

❀ MENTORING ON THE BASEBALL FIELD

"My best friend and I have coached the same Little League team for the past several years," a dad offered. "What that also meant was that our daughters were on our team and we didn't know how that would work. Early on we discovered that if one of us tried to correct our own daughter by telling her to choke up on the bat or throw the ball a different way, our daughter would look at us, roll her eyes, and say, 'Yeah, right.'

"So, we decided to change our strategy. Now, when one of them needs feedback, the other's dad gives it to her." Grinning, he said, "We were both astonished by the reaction. My friend would tell my daughter exactly what I had suggested earlier and she'd listen like it was the word of God and work on it immediately. The same thing," he chuckled, "happened when I gave his daughter feedback." And then, puffing up a little, he said, "We're keeping this a secret for now. But it sure makes us feel like we're good coaches."

❀   TEACHING VALUES

"When our predominantly white Ohio team played a nearly all-black team in a recent football game," a coach was quoted, "racial slurs and trash-talk flew across the line of scrimmage throughout the game. The animosity being built up on the field would tumble over into the parking lots after the game, and fights were common. It was sickening," the coach said. "Rather than file a grievance, we got together with the other coaches and had a pizza night with all the kids. We had a local sports hero give a talk on sportsmanship and share with us his experience in the big leagues. It's really made a difference. But we had to get our priorities in order first." One of the linemen said, "I met a couple of other guys on the opposing team. They weren't all that bad." Another added, "What we should take away from this is that sportsmanship should be elevated above everything else."

FIVE WAYS TO VALUE YOUTH IN SPORTS

1. Meet with parents to review values and expectations. If parents are obnoxious, tell them gently that if they don't knock it off, you'll stop the game.
2. Make a rule: Everyone plays and everyone who wants to be a cheerleader becomes a cheerleader!
3. Find one thing each kid did well during each game and praise him or her for it.

4. Have the kids and adults thank the umpires and opposing team at the end of the game.
5. Run background checks on all coaches to protect our kids. (Most law enforcement agencies will do it for no charge.)

❀

SERVICE ORGANIZATIONS

One of the most overlooked and undervalued assets in our communities are the local service organizations and clubs that generously give whopping amounts of money and time to help kids in the community. But one of the biggest problems service organizations have is that their membership is dwindling each year. One of the keys to reversing this trend is the engagement and involvement of youth with these wonderful organizations. Service club members are perfect mentors for our kids because they "walk the talk."

❀   MEANINGFUL SERVICE

"We really wanted to engage kids in our service club," a local president of a service club in Alberta, Canada said. "It was difficult because we met during school hours, and we weren't sure what to do. One of our members came up with a brilliant idea. He suggested we invite fourth and fifth graders from local schools to come to the club and introduce our speakers. The local schools accepted readily, and now we have kids interviewing our guest speaker two weeks in advance, coming to the meeting all dressed up, telling an anecdote about the speaker, and becoming the hit of the presentation. A national speaker who was introduced by one of the kids affirmed the introduction immediately. 'Absolutely the best introduction I've ever had.'"

❦ LIONS, TREES, AND KIDS, OH MY!

Called the "most passionate tree planter since Johnny Appleseed," Frank Lockyear, the president of ReTree International, says, "There is magic in planting a tree. I sometimes think that placing the seedling in a hole you have dug in the good, rich soil is like handling the tree's spirit. We all share this spirit—it is like a thread that binds us together. Naturalist John Muir once wrote, 'When we try to pick out anything by itself, we find it hitched to everything else in the universe.'"

Frank invites Lions Club members, Boy and Girl Scouts, and kids from the local community to come and help every time his organization wants to retree an area. From Iceland to Thailand to Alaska to Mount St. Helens, this magical combination has resulted in adults and youth working side by side, getting down and dirty, to do something special for Mother Earth.

A Lions Club member from Lake Oswego, Oregon, for over thirty years says about the experience: "Of all the things that we've done as an organization, I think this is one of the most important. We're touching the earth, while kids and those dedicated to creating a better community are working side by side, and there are immediate, tangible results." Smiling, he said, "We're going to invite the kids, the Lions, and all who participated back in a year so they can see how important their work really is."

FIVE IMPORTANT WAYS SERVICE ORGANIZATIONS CAN MAKE YOUTH FEEL IMPORTANT

1. Invite youth to participate in your service work or at fund-raisers and pancake breakfasts.
2. Actively invite youth to join your club or form a youth advisory board to suggest local service projects.
3. Start a training program in your club on how to work effectively with kids. (They may be future members.)
4. Feature youth speakers at weekly meetings.
5. Continue supporting youth efforts by financial contributions.

❁

IN THE MEDIA

In a world driven by powerful images on television, movies, and music videos, youth often look self-obsessed, violent, and downright dangerous. No wonder that a Public Agenda Forum poll in 1997, in which adults were asked if they thought the youth of today would make a positive contribution to society, found that only 37 percent said they thought today's kids, once grown, would make this country a better place.

However, as I travel about the country and talk with kids from all strata of the culture, I see a completely different picture. I hear from bright, articulate kids who want to be actively engaged in changing their communities and the world. Part of encouraging kids to make a difference is to shine the light of local and national media continuously on their hopes, goals, abilities, and achievements. There is much to be highlighted.

So much of life is based on perception. When I was in the tenth grade, I heard a statistic about the number of tenth graders who had had sex. And I remember thinking, "Wow, what's wrong with me?" Rather than focusing on the headline-grabbing aspect of some kids' activities, local and national media could put this generation into perspective by sharing such startling statistics as these, from a 1997 Indiana Children and Adolescent Survey:

72.6 percent of sixth graders have never used cigarettes
77 percent of eighth graders have never used marijuana
83.3 percent of ninth graders have never used inhalants

When we view our kids through this lens, our perspective suddenly shifts. Although there are lots of kids engaged in high-risk behavior, others have decided to abstain from sex, don't drink, and take their lives very seriously. There are many young people who want to be known for their abilities and capacity to make a difference.

❀ YOUTH-DRIVEN MEDIA

Billed as "the nation's only youth-driven communication net-work," a Midwest YMCA proclaims in its mission statement that it involves "youth in year-round positive activities using video and Internet technology to build personal competence and creativity, usefulness, a sense of belonging and empowerment." Youth be-tween the ages of twelve and twenty create a monthly live television program, videotape youth events all over the community, work with media professionals, and write and act in their own comedy show. The director of the program says, "We started by utilizing the public access TV resources and my own outdated camcorder." The key is that the adult staff are "available as professional mentors or coaches rather than lecturers or teachers." Youth participate on their own initiative on projects that are relevant and interesting to them as well as good for the general image of youth in their com-munity. A dedicated core of twelve to eighteen teens is joined by approximately eighty others throughout the year.

If the local and national media started consciously and inten-tionally focusing on what remarkable kids we have and involving them in the communications process, it could create opportunities for future broadcasters to become professionals we respect. We might even begin to see our communities through a different set of eyes.

❀ NEWS OF REMARKABLE KIDS

From a teenager who started an international program to protest child labor abuses in Third World countries, to middle school students who work tirelessly with Special Olympics across the country, to a ten-year-old who, after his first day of classes, told reporters that he hoped they would join him to "walk with him into a century of peace and compassion," our kids are doing remarkable things that we need to hear a whole lot more about. From small to large projects, let's recognize a community, city, county, state, and national kid-of-the-month for their contributions. Once we begin to recognize the gifts these kids have to offer, hundreds of other gifts will come forth, because the kids will not only want to give of themselves, but they will see what is truly important.

PROACTIVE MEDIA TO THE RESCUE

1. Feature kids-of-the-week on local news and in newspapers.
2. Have kids of all ages contribute to local newscasts that highlight school activities.
3. Recognize kids who play an active role in community life: as umpires, on boards, in focus groups at high schools, as great skateboarders.
4. Run a series of articles honoring those who work with kids day in and day out.
5. Support an annual theme of the community's choosing and document it with stories (get to know kids' names, "Say hi to a neighbor," recognize those who work with youth).

❀

IN THE COMMUNITY

A six-year-old boy strayed away from the play area at his day-care center, found a mini-car outside a children's toy shop, hot-wired it, and took off down a busy highway. He was spotted by dumbfounded drivers, who called the police on their car phones. The boy was picked up unhurt.

Although this story strains our credulity, it is true that many adults fail to recognize just how bright and capable kids are. Yet, according to the Search Institute, based in Minneapolis, that has compiled data from over one million kids, only 24 percent of twelve- to eighteen-year-olds across America feel valued by their community, and only 20 percent believe they have a useful community role. At a panel in Orlando, Florida, where teens discussed the challenges they face, I was astonished to hear them complain that they had nothing to do! But as we talked further, I discovered that what these kids were really saying was that there were not enough meaningful roles for them to play in the community. They wanted to be valued, trusted, and respected more than anything else. Today, most parents—like me—earn money, hand it to our kids, and justify our "generosity" by asking them to do a few chores. We are a culture that in many ways has forgotten what to do with our kids, and we all know that under those circumstances, many will find other ways to get our attention.

Kids who feel they have no role to play in their communities suffer from a lack of self-worth. Many will look for other things to fill their lives with, like violence and drugs. One teen at a statewide conference I attended commented insightfully and eloquently: "There are holes in hearts of kids that are being filled with things that make them too heavy to hold."

In order to draw out the energy and genius of our kids, we, as adults need to give up some of our power and allow the kids to try their ideas and to share in the responsibility of their success. The number one complaint I hear from kids who are involved in projects with adults is that the adults try to take over. The second most common complaint is that adults take life too seriously and need to lighten up. We adults always have to remind ourselves that when we undertake a project so our kids can learn responsibility and move into meaningful roles, we must create a balance between the task and building relationships. (And it also helps to have lots of fun and food.) When a balance is struck between these, we all win.

❀   CLASS ACT

Hearing that slavery was being practiced in Sudan, Africa, a group of elementary students in the Midwest decided they wouldn't wait for others to take action. As their teacher watched them mobilize, she said, "Children understand good and bad," and when the kids heard about child slavery in Africa and discovered that for $50 they could free one slave, they sprang into action and, combined with the efforts of others, have freed more than 16,000 slaves. Wanting to make sure that their money was being used for the right purpose, their teacher traveled to the Sudan last summer to see the process in action and to assure the people that the "world has not forgotten about you." Empowered by their success, the students are now raising money for a school and have sent gifts to Sudanese children. But no gift they could ever send would equal the gift that came directly from their hearts—the gift of freedom.

Six-year-old Ryan Helgar of Ontario, Canada, inspired his first-grade teacher to raise funds to build a clean-water well for a village in Africa. Since 1998, Ryan has been working with a national nonprofit organization called WaterCan. Ryan originally set out to raise $70, but after two years the total exceeds $60,000. Ryan will receive a Canadian achievement award for helping to build a culture of peace and nonviolence.

❀   YOUTH TO THE RESCUE

"I couldn't understand how my son could hang out with kids who had pink hair and punk haircuts," a mom from Illinois confided in me. "I told him over and over again, 'Find new friends. You can do better than them.'" Then, tearing up a bit, she said, "One evening, my son was shot and killed in a drive-by shooting as he was leaving a convenience store. He wasn't targeted, he was just in the wrong place at the wrong time. I was devastated and was looking for comfort or understanding from anywhere." Then she paused and said softly, "Do you know who showed up almost every day and who I laughed and cried with? My son's 'punk' friends. We hugged, sat together for hours, and talked about my son. These kids," she continued, "who looked so abnormal on the outside, had so much love to give. They were the ones who helped me through that horrible time." Taking a deep breath, she added, "I had no idea there was so much depth to them. They knew how to 'be there' for me more than most of the adults did."

❀   KIDS AS LEADERS

"I'm a mentor," a high school senior told me. "When I was first asked by our counselor if I'd be interested, I didn't know if I had the skills. But when I understood that what it really meant was that I listen, help a middle schooler with his homework, and maybe shoot some hoops, that sounded like something I could do. I meet with him twice a week as part of a program to connect the high school with the middle school, and the coolest part is when I show up at his class. He introduces me to everybody and treats me like a celebrity. I think," he chuckled, "that his status at school has improved because of me as well."

In an eighteen-month project on reducing violence done by researchers at Northwestern University, youths between the ages of fourteen and twenty-one living in the Cabrini Green neighborhood were recruited as teachers. They helped develop courses that included games, skits, and how to address peer pressures: Kids who were older were admired and listened to, according to the report. After meeting once a week for eighteen months, students were significantly less accepting of violence than those who didn't attend.

Perhaps the unseen impact was summed up by one boy: "I looked up to them." A fifteen-year-old boy said, "They set a good example."

FIVE POWERFUL WAYS WE CAN ENCOURAGE YOUTH TO CHANGE THE CULTURE

1. Remind them that kids who are young see them as their role models.
2. Encourage them to shoot hoops, talk, and say "Hi" to younger kids.
3. Push for school mentoring programs in which older kids teach younger kids.
4. Encourage them to get to know kids from different cliques in school and not to prejudge others!
5. Engage them in efforts to reach out to a senior citizen in the neighborhood who needs help with groceries or cutting the lawn, or who could use some company.

❀ CONNECTING KIDS WITH COMMUNITY RESOURCES

When I was thirteen years old, I had one aspiration in life. I wanted to be a writer for *Mad Magazine.* Satire seemed like a good way to handle a lot of things I didn't understand. I thought the magazine's satires of movies were the most creative pieces I had ever come across. So I spent my spare time thinking up my zingers and creating my own columns. One of my favorite pieces in the magazine was "Snappy Answers to Stupid Questions." As I look back upon that time of my life, I wish someone had recognized this passion, helped me cultivate it, or connected me up with a local writer who could have helped me learn the craft.

A fellow teacher and I were having a discussion about education and we both agreed that the ideal classroom would be a place where basics were covered and then each student could focus on something they were passionate about. But here we hit a snag. We thought, "How will we know what their passions are?" Suddenly it dawned on us—ask them! At that moment, my colleague's seven-year-old daughter came into the room, and we asked, "Liz, if there was one thing you could study in school right now, what would it be?" I was expecting a very long pause, but without missing a beat, Liz calmly replied, "Medicine." After my friend and I recovered, she said, "Liz, how do you know about medicine?" As Liz ran off, she shouted, "I saw a really cool program about it on the Discovery Channel." My friend and I looked at each other like two researchers who had just had personal validation that their theory was correct. "But," we said excitedly, "this would mean a complete change in the way schools do business. The teacher would become as much a facilitator as a pillar of knowledge." But where were the resources to draw upon that would make this a reality? "Hmm . . . ," my friend said. "How about the community?"

❁ TRUE COMMUNITY EDUCATION

What happens when you really reach out to the community as part of the educational process? If you're in British Columbia you may well "Discover Active Living." This simple program can be used in all grades. In one community, it started in elementary and middle schools where students were canvassed to determine what activities they wanted to learn in the practical arts, fine arts, and athletics. Then the expertise of staff, parents, and other community members was matched with the list of activities. When the final menu of activities was established, students selected their top three choices and received six hours of instruction in three different activities for a total of eighteen hours. One six-hour session was offered each season—fall, winter, and spring—in order to take advantage of seasonal activities. For instance, power skating was taught by the principal. Computers and carpentry were taught by a teacher and a senior citizen. Personal grooming was taught by a community member, karate by a local master, sewing by a parent in her home, art by a local artist, Ping-Pong by the vice principal, and radio announcing by a teacher. The coordinator said, "It was absolutely amazing. The adults were so happy because they were sharing something they loved. And it was infectious. The kids now had connections into the community and mentors that really cared about their subject and the kids!"

❀ THE GIFT THAT KEEPS ON GIVING

An eighth-grade boy at a middle school was walking out the door of his science class when his teacher asked him how he was doing. Not knowing anything about his condition, the teacher was shocked when he said, "Not too well; I'm on kidney dialysis three times a week, and I need a new kidney." He explained that 35,000 people were waiting for kidneys and there was only a slim chance he would get one that would work for him. Then it was his turn to be astonished as his teacher said, "I have two kidneys. Do you want one of mine?"

Seeing that she was serious, the boy ran home and proclaimed to his mom, "She's the one, Mom. She always eats fruit or salads all the time!" The boy, who dreamed of playing professional basketball to keep his mind off the fact that he might not live much longer, was suddenly filled with hope. But there still had to be tests to determine if his teacher's tissues matched his, and there was always the possibility that his teacher would reconsider her spontaneous and generous offer.

The teacher was serious, and she went through the tests. The phone call delivering the test results was taken by the nurse. Everyone's heart stopped when she said, "It's negative." But the mood changed in a heartbeat when she sputtered, "But that's good!"

The school's principal, who felt it was divine intervention that the teacher, a white woman, could be a perfect match for a thirteen-year-old black boy, said, "This one, simple act of kindness shows that we're all just alike on the inside." And the tearful mom said, "I've never had someone reach out so far."

❀ NEVER, EVER GIVE UP ON A KID

Taking kids who had not done well in an inner-city high school and awarding them scholarships because they showed promise was a remarkable experiment by the Ladders and Hope program, created by the United Negro College Fund. "These are basically kids who would not have been admitted to any college," said the group's CEO. "It was an experiment to see whether we can take kids with D and C averages and put them in one of our colleges that provided intensive nurturing, mentoring, and monitoring."

Of the forty-seven students who entered the program as of 1999, eighteen have earned bachelor degrees, twelve will graduate in the spring, and four are enrolled in graduate programs. Three have graduated with honors, one left the program and is now a sergeant in the U.S. Army, and only four flunked out. One student said, "The teachers and counselors saw something in me, and they just operated on that." In 1997 she graduated with a sociology degree and is now doing graduate work. Hoping to complete her thesis soon, she looks back at her experience with amazement and says, "If you can ever invest in the idea of potential, it's a risky move. But it can really change someone's entire life, and in some ways, the world."

�֍ YES, VIRGINIA, THERE IS A SANTA CLAUS

What happens to all the letters kids send to Santa Claus each year? With "Operation Santa Claus" at New York City's main post office, miracles happen.

Reminiscent of the movie *Miracle on 34th Street,* stacks of letters are received there each year. They used to end up in dead-mail stacks, unopened and forgotten. But for the past several years, they have been read by business people, grandparents, singles, and others who for a few minutes, sometimes for a few hours, read the letters and pick ones they want to respond to. Some tear up, while others take a more businesslike approach, creating piles of "must respond to" to "maybe will respond to."

One letter from a seven-year-old boy with three sisters between the ages of one and ten asks Santa timidly "for one present they could all share." Another letter comes from a nine-year-old boy who says he, his baby sister, and mom are homeless and he hopes Santa can "send food for his mother and maybe some Pampers and a blanket for his sister." A girl writes, "I live in Coney Island. Do you ever come here?" And yet another boy lists twenty-eight presents he wants and sends pictures so Santa will know exactly what to get.

One reader took thirty letters (she wanted to take more) and spent about $30 on a present for each writer. Even after doing all this, she said she wished she could have done more. "I feel so terrible about the kids who aren't going to get anything for Christmas. It's so tragic." One man who comes year after year to read the letters said he called a mother to make sure it was all right to buy her son the wrestling action figures he wanted. The mother, he said, "started crying and blessin' me" over the phone.

In a world where so many are so materially blessed, it's easy to forget the kids who wake up Christmas morning only to have their hearts broken. But the number of Santas is growing—not only at the New York City post office but in post offices everywhere.

❀ HIGHER GROUND

In Wellesley, Massachusetts, people came together and created a community document that is having a long-term impact. They drew up a town charter whose purpose was to state expectations for kids and other community members and to begin to engage everyone in the process.

One of the participants said, "The charter isn't meant to be a rigid, enforceable set of laws, but a statement of principles. It calls young people to higher standards of behavior in four areas—spirituality, sportsmanship, youth activities, and alcohol and drug abuse—but also urges adults to give clear direction. For example, Wellesley's charter suggests adopting a town-wide statement of sportsmanship signed by players, coaches, and parents.

"The sportsmanship statement calls on players to play hard but follow the rules, and 'treat teammates and opponents alike with kindness.' Coaches are asked to respectfully accept officials' decisions and 'foster in your players a love of the game.' Parents are reminded to 'leave coaching to the coaches.' One concrete result of the charter process—which recommends creating more 'substance-free' recreation opportunities for kids—was Night Shift, a coffeehouse principally run by teens. It drew more than 150 young people on a single night. Another was a determination among charter board members to press for the appointment of a youth panel in city government to look out for young people's interests."

THE TEN TOP WAYS TO SAVE A KID: IN THE COMMUNITY CIRCLE

1. Agree upon common community values and transmit them across the community (on menus, on grocery bags, at schools, at faith organizations, and on sports fields).
2. Begin integrating youth into various levels of community decision-making processes, including committees and boards, and then really listen.
3. Hire a coordinator whose job is not to create anything new but to rewire the community infrastructure, connect the dots, and release community capacity.
4. Create a community vision describing what a community that values kids looks like, sounds like, and feels like.
5. Develop powerful, positive rites of passage for kids, such as performing local service projects with business leaders and participating in service projects to other countries.
6. Become known as a community that puts kids and families first and make efforts to fulfill that vision.

7. Have a community youth day, honoring all those who help youth, publicly recognize them and have youth give out the awards.
8. Integrate kids into roles in the community through which they can learn from adults.
9. Teach adults how to include and how to work effectively with kids.
10. Bring kids together from all groups and ask them how they would use some of the money and resources to create a better place for kids.

SIX

The Fifth Circle:
Business and Government

*In our every deliberation, we must consider the impact of our decisions
on the next seven generations.*

—THE GREAT LAW OF THE IROQUOIS CONFEDERACY

Businesses, corporations, and governmental organizations have
done so much for our children. From sponsoring national
events to local basketball teams, to serving as "cops in the classroom," their involvement with our youth has been vital to creating
healthy communities for our kids. However, as kids increasingly
become a marketing target and source of revenue, businesses and
governmental organizations, including law enforcement, juvenile
justice systems, and local services, need to rethink how their resources can be used even more effectively to support our kids.

Seated next to me on the plane was a woman on her way to a

skiing vacation. She asked me what I did and I filled her in as best I could. As we talked about issues parents face, I commented on the continual raising of the material bar. I used the example of how, when I grew up, birthday parties were composed of cake and games, but how today they have become more like major events. I told her that these days it's not uncommon for kids who go to a party to expect a present for coming to the party! She laughed and said, "You're not going to believe this, but I'm in the product development field and I was on the team that first came up with the whole idea of party themes and favors for birthday parties. It's probably the best idea we ever had." Restraining myself from strangling her, I regained my composure and said, "Do you have any kids?" She shook her head and said, "Nah." At that moment I realized she and I were in completely different worlds. She was so close, but so far away. The challenge was how to bring us together.

❁

THE KID BUSINESS

Parents are under incredible pressure to provide all the material needs that our culture says we and our children must have to be happy campers. As I investigated marketing strategies directed at kids and families, I discovered that corporate America has techniques aimed at creating product loyalty from the moment a child is born. By age two, according to Dan Acuff, author of What Kids Buy and Why, *kids are nagging their folks for the most recent thing they've seen on television. Acuff goes on to say that kids are grouped by ages—birth to two years, three to seven, eight to nine, ten to twelve, thirteen to fifteen, and six-*

teen to nineteen—and that entire campaign ads are directed at each age group. For example, some books that show kids how to count are illustrated with M&M's!

T-shirts imprinted with commercial products are carefully crafted to appeal to children of certain age groups. Kids who wear clothing that sport corporate logos and food advertisements not only provide free advertising, but the parent who buys the T-shirt is paying the businesses for the honor of providing a billboard! A representative for the Center for Commercial-Free Public Education responds to this marketing emphasis by saying, "It's hard to believe so many marketers are sitting around thinking of ways to invade young people's space at a time youngsters are trying to figure out who they are." An entire industry is being built around listening to focus groups of young people and finding out what they want and what the hot new trend will be.

The competition between businesses is so fierce that millions of dollars are spent on gaining loyalty as early as possible and keeping the pressure on. Kids have always nagged their parents to buy products, but today's marketing strategies have raised the stakes and taken it to a whole new level. James McNeal of McNeal & Kids Consulting says kids aged twelve and under spent $27.9 billion of their own money, and influenced $248.7 billion of Mom and Dad's spending in 1999.

Businesses should feel a great responsibility to avoid exploiting our children. Kids, who today wield a lot of economic clout and who have a lot of expendable income, are not simply another sector or percentage share of the marketplace. Honorable businesspeople can create kid-friendly environments rather than kid-exploitative ones. There is an incredible untapped market waiting to be embraced by such astute businesses.

❀ KIDS AS CONTRIBUTORS, NOT CONSUMERS

"Start with low interest rates," the announcement on the envelope addressed to my daughter proclaimed. "Build for the future," it said inside. "Great way for you to start building a positive credit history." So what's wrong with that? Well, I'll tell you: My daughter just turned seventeen! Of course, there are hundreds of items she'd probably like to purchase, but isn't there a bigger question that needs to be asked? How will she pay for them? And that question leads me to another: Don't we have enough people who are in deep trouble because they have been irresponsible about credit? I understand that credit cards are here to stay and that young people need to learn about them, but offering them to teenagers hardly seems to be considering our children's best interests.

As parents, we've got to run interference for our kids. We need to call businesses and ask them to lay off when they've crossed the line. We must also have the ability to follow through—to not use products that we find offensive and to educate our kids about how the products are being sold.

❀ LIVING IN A MATERIAL WORLD

Try this blast from the past:

Think back to when you were growing up and how you thought of two fairly typical items in your closet: blue jeans and tennis shoes. When I was young, we only wore jeans—which were cheap—if we didn't have anything else to wear. Those of us who were lucky had a pair of U.S. Keds in grade school and Converse tennis shoes in high school. Today, as a result of phenomenal marketing, our perception of both jeans and tennis shoes has been greatly altered. We view these two items—both of which are now incredibly expensive—as chic! As a friend of mine put it: "There was a time in America when children wore jeans because their parents were poor. But today parents are poor because children wear jeans." If marketers can do such a good job changing our perception of the value we place on these two items, can't we do that with our kids? Rather than seeing our kids as afterthoughts in our world or a market to be exploited, what if we embraced them as our most important natural resource, to be protected at all costs.

There are a couple of really great ways for businesses to do a reality check and to become socially responsible in the sales of their products. After holding focus groups with kids and finding out what they want to buy, ask focus groups of parents if these products are reasonably priced and in their kids' best interests. Here's a big secret for businesses: Parents want to support products that meet the criteria above. If businesses give parents a reason, they can talk with their checkbooks as well as their feet.

KIDS: MIRRORS OF THE CULTURE

Kids are incredibly impressionable. All the overt and covert messages that adults, businesses, and organizations send through the 20,000 ads kids see every year are internalized, even if the kids do not understand them. Everyone who has worked with kids or who is a parent can tell stories about young people who have misinterpreted some of these messages because of either their youth, their unique experiences, or ignorance. One morning at the breakfast table, a friend noticed that his daughter had a very concerned look on her face. When her dad asked what was wrong, she started crying and said, "Dad, we can't eat breakfast cereal anymore!" When her dad asked why not, she replied, "Because I was watching the news last night and they said there was a cereal killer on the loose!"

As humorous as they are, such stories teach us two important lessons: (1) Our kids may misunderstand many messages, advertisements, and enticements that corporations, business, and the media send out, and (2) our kids are often assaulted with adult ideas that are inappropriate for children. At the very least, we need to be available to interpret those messages for them.

❀

TURNING IT AROUND:
KID-FRIENDLY BUSINESSES

"We had a lot of concerns in our community about the availability of adult material to kids," a New Jersey mom said. "From video jackets with provocative covers, to kids buying a ticket for one movie at the cineplex and then attending any movie they wanted, to billboards with graphic sex depicted on them. We invited the business owners to attend a workshop. We talked a lot about creating kid-friendly environments. One of their 'homework assignments' was for them to go back to their own business environment and review it through the eyes of a child. We asked them to see everything in it as a child might, and if it was the type of message we would want our kids to see.

"Two weeks later, when we reconvened, the grocery-store owner told us excitedly about his experience with the assignment. He said as he walked through the aisles of his store he really didn't see any problems, but when he got to the checkout stand he was dumbfounded. Staring him in the face were magazines and tabloids that were obviously inappropriate. But he said, 'You know, they had been there so long I never thought twice about them.' He told us that, viewing them through his new-perspective eyes, he thought they were totally inappropriate. 'I didn't want to be a censor,' he said, 'so we came up with a whole different approach. We created family checkout lines where there are no magazines, and even no candy! I like to call them the G-rated checkout lines.'"

Continuing, the mom said, "Several really positive things have come of this. The store owner was able to 'alter' the culture right where he was. We tell his story wherever we go. Second, public support for this move has been really positive. There are customers who say they will go out of their way to give their business to a store that puts families and kids first!"

There are many other small, but important, steps that businesses who see a lot of "kid traffic" can take. From video store owners who are putting video jackets with seductive pictures at adult eye-level, to owners of movie theaters and cineplexes who are checking ages more closely when selling tickets and setting up internal checkpoints so kids can't buy a ticket to a G-rated film and then, once past the ticket taker, go to any movie they want—businesses have a responsibility and are recognizing that they are an important piece of any community that wants to create a healthy climate for kids. Kroger, the nation's largest grocery-store chain, announced they will cover up all except the masthead of *Cosmopolitan* magazine, so that its racy covers and cleavage cannot be viewed by everyone who just happens by. It is small acts like this that will change the entire community collage.

❀   BUSINESSES DO LISTEN

A dad who took his daughters shopping was dumbfounded when he saw girls' T-shirts whose slogans were based on slurs directed at girls. One read, "You Play Like a Girl," and another stated, "If I Let You Score, Will You Go Home?" Noting how offended his daughters were by these messages, he complained to two major retailers who carried these products. Within a week, one of them dropped the line. He said, "It's time for dads to speak out on behalf of their daughters."

Daughters who have dads who honor and respect them give them a great gift. According to Jonetta Rose Barras, in her book *Whatever Happened to Daddy's Little Girl?*, "Fathers teach girls how to relate to men and maneuver in a male-dominated society. Fathers help their daughters become comfortable as to who they are as a girl and later as a woman." Columnist William Raspberry agrees. He says, in discussing boys with his girls, "We had the hugest laughs over some of the things guys say to them when they're trying to get over. Some of the lines we used one hundred years ago, they're still saying!"

❀   CYBERSPACE AND SAFE SURFING

With some of the tragic incidents that have occurred involving the Internet, with kids being lured to meet adults after building a relationship in online chat rooms, service provider America Online (AOL) has provided the industry with a fine example of how to engage kids and keep them safe. The company hosts a number of creative channels for kids: a comic-strip club through which kids can create their own comics, a pet picture contest (the winner may become the "pet of the week"), and access to an electronic library through which kids can get help with homework. Through AOL's "Clubhouse," kids get good advice about safety on the Net: Tip Number 5 reads: "Always tell a parent about any bad or threatening language you see, and tell AOL if you get a 'bad' or 'nasty' e-mail message." Celebrities give additional advice on how to "surf safely."

SAFE SURFING TIPS TO SHARE
WITH YOUR KIDS[*]

1. Never provide anyone online, in a chat room, or in an e-mail message with information that would allow them to contact you offline.
2. Never give anyone your password (except your parents).
3. Never, ever agree to meet someone in person without telling your parents.
4. Never respond to bad or threatening language. Report it immediately to your online service and tell your parents or teacher immediately.
5. If you receive strange e-mails, delete them immediately.
6. If someone in a chat room is saying things that make you uncomfortable, leave immediately.

---

[*]Adapted from AOL Kid's Safety Tips.

❀

BUSINESS MENTORING

After doing in-depth research on ways to help kids grow into respon-sible and contributing members of society, an editor of Newsweek *says about mentoring, "Of all of the social ideas of the last thirty years, it's the only one that we know really works." He continues, "No one succeeds in America without some kind of mentor—parent, teacher, coach, older friend—to offer guidance along the way." His be-lief is supported by a study that shows kids who are mentored are half as likely to abuse drugs or alcohol as those who aren't.*

Employees at Newsweek *wanted to be mentors, but the time it took to travel to a school and to return cut too deeply into their workdays. They came up with an innovative idea: The magazine itself became a partner to a middle school. Now every other Tuesday thirteen seventh and eighth graders come to the magazine's offices to talk shop with em-ployees, build relationships, and learn about the world of work.*

The power of mentoring is being documented not only because of its effectiveness but because of its simplicity. A major study by the Harvard Business School indicated that activities like volunteering and mentoring boost employee morale. What a great win-win situa-tion for kids and employers!

❀　WALKING THE TALK

"We really believed in giving back to the kids in the commu-nity," the vice president of a company in Newark, Ohio told me, "but we didn't want to add to our employees' workload. So, after a lot of discussion, we decided to take a leap and instituted a policy that gave all our employees up to seven days off during the work year if they'd volunteer to work with kids in a local program. To sweeten the pot," she said, "we also made it a policy that if they used all seven days, they could take the entire week between Christmas and New Year's as paid time off!

"Has it been successful?" she asked rhetorically. "Well, there's been no one around to answer the phones for the past three years that week!"

❁ WOOING THE YOUNG

Some corporations are going into middle schools and high schools to woo kids to work for them. In a tight labor market, companies are participating in career fairs and are tracking high-achieving kids. "We have found an increasing need to grow a pool of applicants," said a human-resource development specialist from a major company. "In the past we'd recruit from other companies, but that pool is limited." High achievers are invited to visit the company and company representatives visit the students at school.

The good news is that these corporate activities engage schools and businesses in productive ways. Students who are courted are impressed. A high school intern at a large communications corporation commented that being at the company is "a lot like being in physics class, but it's the real world. It's definitely pushed me further toward electrical engineering. And it's really cool and laid back here." Some companies are talking to even younger students. A national employers' representative says, "A lot of employers are going even into middle schools. It's about developing a workforce. There's nothing like name recognition. It's good business."

Business-school partnerships and relationships are vital. But I'd like to encourage businesses to adopt a whole school, mentor as many kids as possible, and seek out not only those who are excelling now, but also those who show an interest and potential. That way we invite all kids to discover what's possible.

❀ SMALL TO MIDLEVEL BUSINESSES GETTING INVOLVED

A representative from an aerospace firm in Boulder, Colorado, as part of an innovative community education program, was shocked when, after his presentation to elementary students, they were so impressed, that they lined up to get his autograph!

In this same community, a high-tech company is releasing employees to spend time as volunteers in schools as teachers, listeners, and links to the real world. One of the business leaders says, "We've been pleased with the caliber of workers in this community—that's why we moved here. But," he continued, "this is a rapidly growing industry with lots of change and we want to keep up. If we can play a role with schools to do that, then we want to play that role."

In a unique collaboration between Boulder schools and businesses, a special program has been created to make sure this connection succeeds. It has three full-time employees, a board of directors, business and foundation support, and the local newspaper as a media sponsor. Their goal is not to create anything new but to link kids up with the powerful resources that are already present in the community.

"I am very much in favor of giving kids a voice in the media," one of the local sponsors, a video production company owner, says. Under the umbrella of this program, he works with three middle schools and helps students learn to write, act, edit, and produce high-quality videos. The owner says, "Kids have a view of their world that is really interesting. I would like to give them a chance to explain and explore their perspective."

❀　KEEPING SAN FRANCISCO BEAUTIFUL

"Before I started working here," a teenage employee of Sunrise Sidewalk Cleaners says, "I was so shy I didn't even want to answer the phone in the office. But now, I have to be sure my salespeople are making their calls, dealing with customer needs, and collecting payments." She emphasized, "What I like is you're always learning things. A woman came one day to teach us how to shake hands."

When asked what she'd be doing if she wasn't working there, the teenager replied, "I'd probably be on the corner like a lot of my friends are. I never thought there was any point going to college, but now I'm sure I'll do that when I leave here. I'm totally committed to it."

What contributed to this remarkable turnaround? A business run by youth—some of whom were gang members. With start-up support from merchants and a small grant from the federal Department of Housing and Urban Development (HUD), these kids are learning the art of entrepreneurship. What do they do? They blast away graffiti and dirt that appears overnight on streets and sides of buildings. Their annual income is $200,000, but the best part is that they employ a lot of kids who are learning to take care of and restore their community.

FIVE IMPORTANT WAYS BUSINESSES
CAN HELP KIDS AND FAMILIES

1. During annual company picnics, recognize the largest families, those that win a game as a team, or those that have the oldest members.
2. Hold lunchtime workshops that feature tips for working parents.
3. Declare a discount day for families at your business.
4. Feature family-related articles in your company newsletter.
5. Sponsor needy families in the community by holding or contributing to a food, clothing, or holiday gift drive.

❀

COMMITTED TO OUR YOUTH

In the 1500s, the famed Iroquois Confederacy, composed of seven Indian nations located in the Northeast, achieved a level of democracy that in many ways has been unequaled in history. It gave every individual a vote in tribal decisions, and because babies were too young to vote, mothers with children had two votes. Voting for themselves and on behalf of their children, mothers generally carried the day. With remarkable foresight, the Iroquois looked at every decision they made and the impact of those decisions on the next seven generations. Children and families were viewed as the backbone of the community.

The encounters our kids have with judges, police, firefighters, juvenile justice officers, and local governmental employees can have a big impact on their lives. Realizing the importance of their role, local government and city service employees are reconsidering the way they interact with kids. Many of them are going out of their way to change their relationships with young people. Those of us who dial 911, who have had our kids picked up by police, and who have stood with them in front of a judge have also seen that how they are treated and perceived has a huge impact on their lives. These people ought to be encouraged to continue their commitment to our youth.

❀   KID-FRIENDLY COURTHOUSES

"Some parents who had to appear in court," a lawyer in Orlando, Florida, said, "would have to bring their kids with them. But quite often," he continued, "they didn't want their children hearing what they were being charged with, so they'd leave their kids outside the courtroom in the hallways. This," he said emphatically, "is not the place where you want to leave a child!" Lawyers and court employees got together and created a staffed child-care room where kids could watch a video, read quietly, or talk with the staff member about how they felt coming to a courthouse. "Now," the lawyer says proudly, "we've taken a big load off the parents, and, hopefully, turned what could have been a pretty scary situation for a child into one that looks out for their best interests."

❀ JUVENILE JUSTICE TURNAROUND

"You know," a juvenile justice officer said, "all of us in this work have known for a long time that we had to work with the kids that we were seeing in a different way. I mean, by the time a kid got to us we would know everything bad this kid had done, and the laundry list was so long, it really colored the way we saw and worked with these kids. One day, we embarked on a whole new approach. Rather than trying to fill in all the holes in their lives, we decided to find out what they really liked to do, what their strengths were, and create a personal plan around that rather than just slot them into a program and attempt to fill up their holes. Here's an example," he offered. "It may not sound like a big deal, but it is for us. We now interview kids when they enter our world and find out what they really like. One kid who had just entered the system said he really enjoyed working on hot, cool cars. Finding this out, the officer working with him immediately took him on a stroll through the parking lot and asked him 'What's a hot, cool car to you?' The boy picked out three, and one of them was owned by a juvenile justice officer." Chuckling, he said, "Guess who became his mentor? And you know what they talked about for the first month? Hot, cool, cars. We've decided that we need to build the relationship first, and then the rest will follow."

❀ POLICE AND RETAILERS: JOINING FORCES

A police officer in Texas approached me excitedly after a presentation I had given and said, "I want to show you this." Pulling out a manual, he said excitedly, "We're putting something together here that is really taking off." As he turned the pages, his eyes lit up. "It started when those of us on the force started seeing a lot of kids getting high on inhalants they had bought at local stores. Some of these kids were so young and so whacked out that it was really frustrating because we thought there was nothing we could do. Venturing into uncharted waters, we decided to go to local business owners and ask them to refuse to sell a list of inhalants to kids. We called it 'responsible retailing,' and we didn't know how they'd respond. But all of them thanked us for sharing the list and asked to be updated as the 'inhalant of the month' changed. They also agreed not to sell them to the kids!" Excited, he continued, "We're now talking to store owners about other things—like skateboarding, kids hanging out in front of their stores—and we've all started working together on behalf of our kids."

❈ SO LITTLE, SO MUCH

"A friend of mine in law enforcement in Camarillo, California, had been pestering me for a long time to join the force," a guy about my age told me. "But I had a good job as a headhunter, and changing occupations in midlife didn't sound all that appealing. However," he smiled, "I wasn't making the difference I thought I could, so I made the leap. Most of my friends said I was crazy and that I'd regret it, and although I made it through all the training and was assigned to be a liaison officer at a school attended by kids who were on the edge of dropping out, for a while I had a sinking feeling I had made the wrong decision. But something happened that proved my gut instinct right. Oftentimes, I'd sit at the lunch table with the biggest, baddest kids and just say, 'What's up?' They really didn't know what to make of me. I was as old as some of their dads! One afternoon," he continued, "I set up a volleyball game be-tween two gangs, and when they found out how good I was, they both wanted me on their team." Then, pausing, he said, "But the real payoff came when I least expected it. My daughter asked me one day if I knew a kid named Enrique at the continuation school. I said sure, we play volleyball and joke around together. 'Well,' my daughter said, 'his girlfriend goes to my school and she says En-rique told her that you are his best friend.' I was so startled by her comment I didn't know what to say, but it suddenly dawned on me that maybe I was making the difference I really wanted." As he headed toward his squad car he looked back and with a wink said, "Changing jobs is one of the best things I've ever done."

❀ COOL COP IN HOT WATER

"One of my first calls as a police officer," a twenty-year veteran said, "was to respond to the crime of 'road hockey' in progress in a cul-de-sac. I was fresh out of training and ready to take on the world. In what I thought was a smooth move, I blocked off the cul-de-sac so no other traffic could flow through, turned on the red and blue flashing lights and marched up to the kids. I was in full uniform," he laughed, "and I could see the kids shaking in fear as I approached.

"'I have a complaint that you are using the road for hockey,' I said, noticing the kids were nervous. 'There are two ways to go on this. I can shut you down so you don't get run over, or I leave my car where it is and we play. Got an extra stick?' We played for forty-five minutes. During that time we talked about drugs, the law, and the cool things that cops get to do. I was feeling pretty good about my-self that day—I made a whole bunch of friends and I was pretty positive that I had really made a difference in a few lives." Hesitating, he said, "However, my bubble burst the next day when my boss hauled me into his office. Apparently, the person who complained about this road hockey game also made an official complaint against me for neglect of duty. My pleas went nowhere with my boss or the complaining citizen—they didn't understand that it was more important to make a connection than trot out the provincial traffic act."

❀   BEAT THE HEAT

"Cruising on weekends happens in almost every community across the country," a Southern California policeman said. "And inevitably, where there is drinking and car racing, somebody gets hurt or killed.

"We wanted to come up with something creative that still allowed the kids a way to hang out and cruise, but in a safe way," he continued. "So, in a dramatic move, we invited the kids to race at the local racetrack on weekends where they can even challenge a cop to a race. On weekends for the past three years," he continued, "hoods are up, and we compare engines, talk shop, and build relationships. Above all, safety is stressed, but they can challenge us to a race if they want. They usually win," he said with a smile.

FIVE KEY WAYS TO CONNECT LAW ENFORCEMENT WITH KIDS

1. Eat lunch with kids at school and play with them at recess.
2. Start a "responsible retailing" initiative, which encourages retailers to monitor closely what they sell to kids.
3. Help residents connect with Neighborhood Watch programs and with each other through telephone trees. Encourage them to get to know the kids (by name) on their block.
4. Create advisory boards for kids and consult them for input, support, and communications.
5. Connect kids on the edge with service organizations.

❀   NOT BUSINESS AS USUAL

"At our firehouse," an excited fireman told me, in Gillette, Wyoming, "we're committed to helping at-risk kids. We started by teaming up with a school and as part of their school time they were 'assigned' to the firehouse. After teaching these kids how to use some of the equipment, we had them help feed us hoses while we were fighting grass fires. I was amazed to see their self-confidence build as we worked with them. You could see the change taking place in the way they saw themselves. One day they were outlaws with no compass, but before they knew it, they were side by side with firemen, and they knew we were depending on them for the help.

"After putting out the fires, we'd sit and talk about 'most everything," he said. "Their response was incredible. They were so proud of themselves for their contribution, and some of these kids have already decided that they want to pursue firefighting as a career. We've been able to make a little difference in their lives, but what really makes us feel good is when some of the kids we've worked with over the years drop in and want to tell us about their new girlfriend or just shoot the breeze."

❀   UTILITY TRUCKS TO THE RESCUE

If a kid needs help in a Georgetown, Texas, community, all they have to do is look for one of the fifty or sixty utility trucks that are in the field all the time, and all they need to do is ask one of the utility truck workers for help. The Water Services Department says, "We have radios that can contact police, fire, and EMT services immediately." All the utility workers have been trained in how to respond to a kid who needs help.

To assure the children's safety, background checks have been done on all the workers, and to personalize the program, a contest was held to pick the best logos designed by students in two middle schools that are proudly displayed on all the trucks. In addition, the utility drivers go to the schools on a yearly basis to talk with the kids and to acquaint them with their purpose. "The servicemen love working with the kids," the water manager says. "And the program is a hit across the community."

THE TEN TOP WAYS TO SAVE A KID:
IN THE BUSINESS AND GOVERNMENT CIRCLE

1. Place a positive community-belief statement about kids in the window of your establishment (whether private or government)—and act on it every day.
2. Consider the impact of your image and media messages on young people before using them.
3. Teach your teen employees with positive feedback.
4. Give employees time off to work with a local youth-serving organization.
5. Set aside a "bring your kid to work" day and provide a tour that shows them how you operate.
6. Create a mentoring program for kids. Invite them on a regular basis to "shadow" an adult for a few hours.
7. Help create places for kids to meet that are safe (mall snack shops or drop-in centers where there is an adult who can listen to kids).
8. Review your organization through the eyes of a young person to see what sort of messages it is sending to youth.
9. Rethink your policies and procedures: How can they be more accommodating to kids and their families?
10. Ask yourself and your colleagues: What are we trying to do as an organization and how can we help involve or serve youth as part of our mission?

SEVEN

The Sixth Circle: Our Elders

Let me share a Sioux word, tiospaye, *which means the people with whom one lives. . . . The* tiospaye *gives children multiple parents, aunts, uncles and grandparents. It offers children a corrective factor for problems in their nuclear families. If parents are difficult, there are other adults around to soften and diffuse the situation.*
—MARY PIPHER, *THE SHELTER OF EACH OTHER*

When I was nineteen years old I had an encounter with my step-grandmother. It all began when I started doing a few jobs for her, and when I was finished we'd have tea and cookies. Before I knew it, we were sharing stories and learning we had some of the same interests and questions about life. We began to develop a close bond. I'd share a book with her that I had read, and she'd tell me what she thought of it. It was a give-and-take relationship, and we discussed the big issues of life: spirituality, life after death, and following your path.

I had never had such an experience with an elder before. She and I had a kinship, an exchange of ideas, and a bond that transcended age. I remember how much I looked forward to our talks and how she'd light up when she opened the door and saw me. As I look back upon it, the experience was unique, but one that I wish had occurred by design rather than chance. In many cultures that are successful in raising children, it is the role of elders to engage youth in discussions. An incredible fabric of mutual respect is woven. I discovered someone who was asking the same big questions I was, and the only difference between us was about forty years.

❀

THE MISSING CONNECTION

Across America, kids are growing up without the vital connection with wise elders. Dr. Urie Bronfrenbrenner states the need for this connection passionately when he says, "Every young person in America should have at least six adults in their life who are absolutely crazy about that kid." They show up at soccer games. They remember birthdays. They are present for important rites of passage, and by being there they become a significant voice, guide, and advocate for that young person.

These significant adults, whether they are grandmas, grandpas, aunts, uncles, coaches, or family friends, are there to help the parent and to provide guidance when needed. In many cultures of the past, the role of this trusted adult or wise elder was highly revered, and their presence considered essential if the community was to thrive. But according to an attitudes and behaviors survey conducted by the

Search Institute, which has surveyed more than one million twelve- to eighteen-year-olds, the number of significant, trusted adults the average American child in that age group has outside of their parents is less than one!

✿   AGE SEGREGATION

"My parents have lived in Sun City, Arizona, for the past seven years," a mom said, "and my sister and I were getting worried because they were becoming more and more close-minded and judgmental toward their own grandchildren. However, when I spoke with my sister last night, she told me that there had been a major breakthrough. Dad was eating breakfast at the club and he overheard a woman talking to a friend. The woman said, 'I told my son he's welcome to come for Christmas, but if he thinks he's bringing that kid of his with the baggy pants and spiky hair, he should just stay home!' Dad told my sister that he was stunned because he had suddenly heard himself talking and he didn't like it. He called her up to tell her, 'I want you to know . . . you and all your kids are welcome to come visit at any time.'"

In some of Arizona's senior citizen communities you can own a dog or a cat, but you can't have a kid! In one of the communities, the council fined a couple $100 a day who took in a grandkid who claimed abuse by a stepfather. Although a compromise has been sought, the mentality behind it is scary.

Grandparents, elders, and caring adults with wisdom to share are needed within every circle of our communities. Their words can oftentimes be far more powerful than those of parents. Kids who see their parents every day, and who can become deaf to their parents' pleas, will listen to grandparents who adore and respect them.

MISSING IN ACTION

"I get ten phone calls a week from parents who are looking for grandparents for their kids," says the coordinator of a Foster Grandparents program in Missoula, Montana. "When they hear that we provide services only for foster kids who need grandparents, they are deeply disappointed. These parents," she observed, "are looking for wise elders to help teach, guide, and mentor their kids." In many traditional cultures it was an honor to be the guide, the voice of wisdom, and the mentor for future generations. Adults were present to provide apprenticeships, to mentor the young and to perform or witness vital rites of passage into the world of adulthood. Some adults actually would exaggerate their age because it would bring them more respect and honor.

Where are these adults today? Gone! They're trucking down to Florida, flying to California, or moving to Arizona looking for the good life. In our highly mobile culture, in which the average American family moves every seven to nine years, our kids do not experience long-lasting connections with adults in the personal circle of their lives. This loss has a tragic impact on our kids and our culture.

The extended family is a distant memory for most of us. In 1950, 50 percent of all American families had grandparents in or near home. That usually meant that some other significant members were somewhere close as well. That percentage today is less than 10. We should turn that deficit around and ask the question that will lead us to restore this important asset or strength; "How can we cultivate the resource of significant trusted adults in our own backyards and create powerful intergenerational experiences across the entire spectrum of our community?"

✿

GRANDPARENTS STEPPING UP

In the midst of grandparents who are hundreds of miles away, more and more grandparents are becoming "parents" again. Due to their own children's drug habits or having to move home, a Census Bureau report in 1999 indicated that 3.9 million children in the U.S. were living in homes maintained by grandparents. That's up 75 percent since 1970.

The actor George Kennedy and his wife adopted their five-year-old granddaughter. Although he's seventy-five and his wife is sixty-eight, he says, "As grandparents, we have so much more time to spend with her. So, even though we aren't so nimble as young parents, we're around for Taylor and can give her the attention she needs. We are elderly parents, and she is the light of our eyes."

✿   RECONNECTING THE AGES

"We had a major public relations problem," a principal told me. "We had just opened an alternative high school for kids at risk in a neighborhood of nearly all senior citizens. They all had lobbied hard not to have the school here, so we felt like we were walking on eggs. When an early snowstorm hit the area, we had a great idea. We rushed out and bought as many snow shovels as we had kids and teachers, and we shoveled all the walks in the neighborhood for the next several hours. The senior citizens and neighbors were so delighted," said the principal, beaming, "that they showed up with cookies the next day. We now have a stream of community members who come in and work with the students."

From high school students who are showing citizens in retirement homes how to use the Internet to access health-care information to schools that are holding combined senior student–senior citizens dances, to senior citizens who are being invited into the schools to read to the kids, the reconnection is occurring in many grassroots ways.

❀   THE TEDDY BEAR RELATIONSHIP

"Many years ago, one of the programs I implemented in our Zanesville, Ohio, junior high school was called Adopt an Elder," a teacher said. "I collaborated with the local county retirement home and made arrangements for junior high students to visit the elderly. Two days a week I took four to six students to the home. They helped the elderly with exercises, read mail to residents, played cards, or shared stories with them.

"The principal had decided that student eligibility for this program would be based on grades and positive behavior, but I felt that several students who weren't deemed eligible would benefit greatly. On my own time I began to visit the home with one of these other students whose name was Johnny. Johnny was considered the 'loser of the year' at school, but he really wanted to help the seniors. Johnny quickly became a great asset and immediately formed a relationship with Margaret, a ninety-five-year-old woman who seldom received any visitors. Margaret, who was born in Germany, had many experiences to share. Johnny started visiting her on his own, but one Saturday he accompanied Margaret and the residents to the County Fair. When he won a teddy bear at one of the booths, he gave it to her. Months later, Margaret became gravely ill. As she lay clutching her 'Johnny Bear,' Johnny sat quietly with her until she died. The boy who had been written off as a loser had a very big gift to give. He has grown up to be a fine young man, and now he visits me with his son."

❀   AGELESS MAGIC

A retired Eugene, Oregon, pipe fitter who always wanted to learn to play the French horn tried a few adult classes. But they were too advanced, so he courageously asked the local middle-school music teacher if he could play with the school band. The teacher, who at first was taken aback, considered his request and took this "new kid" under his arm and introduced him to all in the band. The pipe fitter was met with both open giggles and admiration, and not long afterward, intergenerational harmony was heard in the halls. Music in this case transcended age, and the band members found a soul mate who was a source of inspiration, guidance, and—when he played his horn—humor.

❀

INVITING YOUTH INTO THE CIRCLE OF WISDOM

Our kids yearn to be included in the circle of wisdom with adults. Within these "circles," which can be conversations, meetings, or mentorships, our kids are like sponges absorbing all we have to share.

✿   BUILD IT AND THEY WILL COME

"I proposed to our congregation that we build a basketball court behind the church for the kids of the community," a minister in a coastal town in Oregon said. "At first, the congregation protested. 'Why should we?' they asked. 'We can't use it and it won't get kids to church!' 'We do need it,' I replied, 'because the kids in this community belong to all of us, and when you think about it, our community is pretty small and there isn't that much for kids to do.' That argument," he smiled, "and me being the minister, did it.

"We decided to build a court with some unique features. There was no fence around the court, so that it would be inviting, and the basket was adjustable, so 'most anybody could play or—even better for the shorter kids—dunk! We also decided on having a light so the kids could play at night. Almost immediately it began to pay off. My wife and I, who lived next to the church, could hear the *ka-chunk* sound of the basketball over and over as more and more kids started showing up to shoot hoops. That sound became music to our ears.

"One evening it was really late, and, hearing the *ka-chunk*, I looked out the kitchen window, and my eyes met those of an anxious boy, who probably thought I was going to ask him to leave because of the hour. But instead, I waved and smiled. He waved and the *ka-chunk* continued. I figured he had a good reason to be there, and there were a lot riskier things he could be doing than shooting hoops."

❀ RETHINKING OUR PRIORITIES

"I had been the cook at the annual Boy Scout Jamboree in the Upper Peninsula of Michigan for the past twenty years," a health-care worker told me. "For the first several years," he said, "I really enjoyed having the scouts help out in the kitchen while we prepared meals for the hundreds of participants. But as the time went by, it was much easier to do all the preparation, cooking, and clean-up with just a handful of adults. After all, when it was just the adults I didn't have to deal with cut fingers, dirty hands on the food, organizing dishwashers, and all the accompanying shenanigans.

"But one day it dawned on me that the purpose of the activity was not just to get the food served, but to work with the kids, let them help, and to build relationships with them. So, we've gone back to the old days, dirty hands and all! What the heck," he said, laughing at himself. "Dirty hands, cut fingers, and all are worth it. And when you come to think of it," he said with insight, "the Jamboree is for them—not for me!"

❀ ELDERS TO THE RESCUE

"You'd be surprised how many friends you lose because they don't want to be around kids," a grandmother from Independence, Missouri, said. How does she know? This grandmother and her husband, foster parents for almost twenty years, have taken care of ninety-seven foster children as well as raised five of their own.

The husband, a former store manager, says, "It gives you a sense that maybe you're helping, making a difference. You have to love them—this has to be a labor of love, or you wouldn't do it."

In their modest three-bedroom home, the walls are covered with photos of "their" kids and their own grandchildren. However, there are some downsides. "Our own kids think we're crazy," his wife says. "I cry a lot; it hurts, but you learn to go on." But her husband adds, "It kind of brings you back to your youth. It's like I'm thirty-five years old again."

FIVE DON'TS FOR ELDERS WHEN IT COMES TO KIDS

1. Don't allow the "costume of the day" to put you off.
2. Don't purposely avoid kids.
3. Don't hesitate to tell kids a story.
4. Don't be afraid to be a "character" once in a while—give a kid some good sound advice when you have the chance.
5. Don't think they won't listen to advice or seek you out for help if you offer it.

THE POWER OF STORY

Throughout history, the values, beliefs, and principles of the cultures have been transmitted to the young through teaching, modeling, and storytelling. But to tell stories, we must have storytellers, and they must have opportunities to tell their stories.

In Ireland and Scotland there is a tradition called Ceilidh *(pronounced "kaley"), during which the community gathers on a regular basis to sing songs and tell stories. The elders play an important role in this process as they pass on the stories of their past and of the community.*

Many traditional communities had one or several "keeper of the stories" who would pass the culture on around the campfires. Stories were told again and again, and the young were groomed to carry on this tradition. Richard Stone, in The Healing Art of Storytelling, *suggests that we prime the pump by asking our elders to begin to share stories that are connected with historical events in their lives, such as their birthdays, the stock market crash of 1929, the Great Depression, the bombing of Pearl Harbor, D-Day, their marriage days, where they lived or served during World War II, the Korean War, the Kennedy-Nixon television debates, the Cuban missile crisis, and a host of other events.*

❀　　**TALKING STORY**

"Being a Native Hawaiian," a presenter at a conference said, "my mom had a unique job at a resort on Kauai. Her job was to walk around the resort in full Hawaiian garb and 'talk story.' She would tell visitors about the island, the ancient myths, and the significance of the rituals and dances they would see at night."

On a Native American reservation in the Southwest, kids are interviewing the elders and capturing their life stories on videotape. These stories, once close to being lost, are now a living library of the past for generations to come. Not only are the elders honored by being asked to tell their fascinating stories, but the young are doing the community a great service by capturing them. Talking story is a powerful way to connect us and our kids with our roots and with other cultures.

❀ INTERGENERATIONAL BONDING

This ad appeared in a county newspaper in Ohio:

Twice a month adult and adolescent women will be getting together to hang out, have fun, make friends, and talk. The purpose? To establish trusted adult relationships with adolescent girls ages 11–14 that will build them up and empower them to make wise choices and become successful women. Please consider becoming a Circle of Friends mentor if any of the following apply to you:

- you respect and like youth
- you want to give young women the stability you had as an adolescent
- you want to help young women deal with the confusion and/or pain you felt as an adolescent
- you have raised healthy, happy daughters
- you have always wanted a daughter
- you have learned from mistakes in raising your

own children that you can use in helping other adolescents
- you believe that there are no bad kids, just bad choices
- you feel like you have something to give to the community
- you want to make a difference in the life of a young woman
- you want to see young women achieve
- you are concerned about pregnancy, drug use, lack of self-esteem, lack of self-discipline, lack of direction, and lack of goals among young women

THIS IS YOUR CHANCE TO
DO SOMETHING POSITIVE!

Bringing our elders and kids together in creative ways will reconnect two of the most powerful resources we have in our own backyard—the enthusiasm, optimism, and innocence of our youth, and the wisdom, pragmatism, and experience of our elders.

FOUR GREAT WAYS TO BE
AN EXCEPTIONAL ELDER

1. Join a seniors club and "adopt" kids who need attention and help.
2. Become a Big Brother or Big Sister.
3. Talk positively about kids in your community to friends.
4. Pick a kid who works at a local business you go to often, and ask them about their job and plans for the future.

❀

RITES OF PASSAGE

Flying in and out of Salt Lake City for years, I witnessed on numerous occasions young and old in droves waiting with balloons and banners for someone getting off the plane. After inquiring, I learned that the grand receptions were for kids who were members of the Church of Latter-Day Saints who were returning from their two-year missions. On one trip, I found myself seated next to one of the kids who was just beginning his mission. I asked him where he was going, how much it cost, and how long he'd be gone. Excited, he told me he was going to Sweden for two years and that he had saved $10,000 during the past six years from his paper route in order to go!

About thirty minutes into the flight, another dimension of this important rite of passage occurred. A beaming woman in her forties came to the back of the plane and said to the group, "Over twenty years ago I went on a mission . . ." I glanced at the kids she was talking to. Their eyes were glued to her. They absorbed her every word. They sat transfixed as she told them her story and ended by saying how proud she was of them. And in that moment I wished this same or a similar experience for my own kids: a powerful rite of passage that they anticipated and saved for, and that would be a signature experience for them the rest of their lives.

Throughout history, it has been the job of elders to provide youth with powerful rites of passage into their community life. As part of these rites, stories of the community and vision quests would be told to the young by the elders. Many cultures are rich with rites of passage from adolescence to adulthood. Jewish bar and bat mitzvah ceremonies recognize the adult status of young men and young women who have studied and are ready to assume their spiritual responsibility in the community. Latino traditions call the coming-of-age ritual for young girls quinceañera, *and mark it with a spiritual blessing and the involvement of friends and older adults in the community.*

What rites of passage do our youth have? For too many kids today, the rites of passage into adulthood are getting high, getting drunk, getting a driver's license, or having sex. Surely there are better ways.

❀ BLESSING THE CHILDREN

"We really need rites of passage for our kids," a grandparent shared with *Spiritual Elder Magazine.* "In the past, cultures have had rites or ceremonies that affirm the coming of age, the passing on of wisdom, and the taking on of more responsibility by a young man or woman." Smiling, he continued, "I even have an example." Pulling a newsletter from his pocket, he read us this story:

"It was a perfect October evening—cool and crisp with a full moon," said an elder about a blessing ceremony for two twin boys. "We sat before a blazing fire surrounded by boulders and pine trees. I arranged the group, by age, in a circle around the fire: eleven men ranging in age from thirty-five to sixty, the two twins, and their friends, ages thirteen and eighteen. When the circle was complete, the eldest and youngest were seated side by side.

"My friend," he continued, "who was the father, stood and spoke first. He told each of his sons how much he loved them, how much they meant to him, and he described his awe at watching them mature. He questioned them about the meaning of manhood. The rest of the men joined him with words of encouragement, songs, poems, and gifts. The air was filled with laughter, music, and an awareness of this special ritual.

"For the elder blessing, the mood became quiet and solemn. I removed two small leather pouches from my jacket pocket, each one containing a piece of obsidian (a black, volcanic glass), and I explained its significance. Then we passed the pouches around, and either silently or with spoken words, put a blessing or wish in each pouch. The boys received blessings for responsibility, trustworthiness, humor, loyalty, appreciating their feminine side, and for allowing their male side to grow.

"That night," he said, "I was reminded that sitting in a circle with elders helps us realize how we all pass through the cycles and stages of our lives. Not only was the campfire ceremony a profound experience for the twins, but the men in the group remarked they had benefitted also."

❀ THE POWER OF RECOGNITION

"There is a very distinguished older man in our congregation," a churchgoer said. "His children are grown and there are several grandchildren. You probably know people like this retired couple: generally healthy, quiet, willing to help out in the background— definitely not interested in anything that would require them to be very public.

"One Sunday when I was in the kitchen of our church, this gentleman came in looking for one of the youth. 'Seen the Smith kid?' he asked, just as the middle Smith boy walked into the room. 'You are just the person I'm looking for!' he said to the teenager. 'I saw your name in the paper last week!'

"The teen looked puzzled. 'You know, for being on the honor roll! You just keep up the good work there. Congratulations!' he said before he turned around and headed for worship. The teen looked at me . . . and he *grinned!* 'I didn't think anybody but parents read those lists—the print's so small!' he said.

"All through worship the middle Smith boy grinned, and once in a while he looked over at the gentleman. When it was time to share the peace, and even though he was almost across the room, that teen made it a point to be where he could shake hands with his newest cheerleader."

THE TOP TEN WAYS TO SAVE A KID:
IN THE CIRCLE OF OUR ELDERS

1. Encourage and pray for kids whether they're near or far.
2. Help develop meaningful rites of passage for them.
3. Take a grandkid to dinner or invite one to have milk and cookies.
4. Be a secret helper for a kid who needs help (pay for music lessons, a sports uniform, etc.).
5. Get your service club to work with kids on a project that is kid-oriented (paint a mural or build a skate park).
6. Think back to the way you used to dress and accept the fact that styles change. (Tell your grandkids what was considered "wild" when you were young.)
7. Hold an intergenerational dance in your neighborhood, community, church, or synagogue. (Swing is back!)
8. Be proud to be an elder and encourage your friends to build relationships with kids.
9. Go out of your way to congratulate kids in your neighborhood or congregation if you read or hear something positive about them.
10. Talk about important moments in your life: getting married, going to war, moving across the country.

EIGHT

The Courage to Commit

It's the action, not the fruit of the action that's important. You have to do the right thing. It may not be in your power, may not be in your time, or that there'll be any fruit. But that doesn't mean you stop doing the right thing. You may never know what results come from your action. But if you do nothing, there will be no result.

—MAHATMA GANDHI

A father and mother brought their son to Mahatma Gandhi and asked him to tell their son to stop eating sugar. Gandhi thought for a moment and said, "Come back in three days." Three days later the excited parents came back with their son. Looking the boy squarely in the eye, Gandhi said to him, "Stop eating sugar." Stunned, the parents inquired, "Why did you tell us to come back after three days? You could have told him that when we first arrived!" Gandhi replied, "I had to stop eating sugar first before I could tell him to quit."

The essential shift starts with each of us. It begins when a personal truth resonates so clearly that we glimpse, perhaps for but a moment, a vision, or a new possibility. When we are willing to take a leap of faith based upon a powerful personal truth, everything begins to change. Every time someone somewhere acts upon a personal truth through a small act of courage, the world is changed. When we begin to take these truths into our organizations, institutions, and communities, and as we begin to align these truths with our policies, the process of change will ripple through all our circles of influence. This is true power. This is what will transform our environment.

In chapter 1, I shared Confucius's philosophy for bringing about change through a systems approach. However, the second part of his philosophy is rarely quoted, though it brings us full circle once again to the power and importance of the individual. He states:

Having sought true knowledge in the soul
They became sincere in their thoughts.
Their thoughts sincere, their hearts were changed.
Their hearts changed, the persons were transformed.
The persons transformed, the families were well regulated.
The families well regulated, the states were well governed.
The states well governed, the kingdom was at peace.

It's my hope that, after we have journeyed through the six circles of community gathering inspiration and wisdom from others, we can each reaffirm our commitments as individuals to change our communities and our culture. Change always begins right where we are, but with new ideas and new eyes. T. S. Eliot eloquently captured this notion in *Four Quartets* when he wrote: "And the end of all our exploring will be to arrive where we started and know the place for the first time."

It all begins by starting "small." When we begin to think small, we can become much like a master weaver who is asked to create a beautiful tapestry. First the weaver envisions the finished tapestry, seeing it in all its future beauty. Then, beginning with a single thread, the magic begins to flow from the weaver's hands onto the tapestry. Some of the threads are thick and colorful, while others are more discreet, yet each thread in the tapestry is essential to the project. So it is within our community tapestry. There's the beautiful baby at the grocery store we can smile and wave to. There are the kids (who used to be annoying) skateboarding down the street, who we now understand are just being kids. And there's the girl with Down's syndrome that we don't avoid, but whom we engage and from whom we maybe even get a hug! When we consider each small thread in the community tapestry as essential, we start seeing things differently. Mother Teresa summed it up beautifully when she said: "We can do no great things, but we can do small things with a great amount of love."

"Years ago," a columnist stated, "I would see this guy walking around town with a tiny, elderly, frail-as-a-bird woman. He could have been her caretaker, but something about the way they clung to each other told me they were mother and son.

"He was in his early thirties or so and had the sweet, innocent countenance of a saint, I thought, or maybe even an angel. Tall, thin, dressed in khakis and a baseball cap, he towered over her, one hand supporting her arm, the other around her back, matching his long stride to her tiny shuffle.

"They made quite a pair. I was so taken with them, I was tempted to offer them a ride. But I was always in a hurry with a minivan full of kids. I let the opportunity pass.

"One day I saw him walking alone and I knew I had missed my chance; I would never meet her. After that, I didn't see him again and pretty soon I forgot all about him. Or maybe I just chose not to remember. Either way, I was surprised recently to cross paths with him again.

"Once again, I almost walked away. But sometimes you feel a longing—a need to know—that later you'll look back on as a calling.

"'Excuse me,' I said, introducing myself. 'I used to see you walking with an elderly woman and I wonder, well, how is she doing?' His name was Ernie, he said, as he shook my hand. His mother, he said, had had Alzheimer's disease. He and his father had cared for her at home, mortgaging the house to pay medical bills. She died two years ago, he said, and a year later, he lost his dad. When the bank wanted to foreclose, Ernie sold the house, paid off the debts, and rented a small place he shares with a roommate.

"It was hard losing his parents, he said. 'Did you ever lose someone?' he asked.

"'My husband died two years ago,' I told him. 'He was a teacher at Monterey High School.'

"'I went to Monterey High,' he said. 'What was his name?' When I told him, Ernie's face lit up. 'I knew your husband. I had him for math. He was a good teacher. He got me to go to Young Life. I liked it so much I went every week.'

"I laughed, remembering how my husband loved playing guitar for Young Life, a Christian outreach program for high school kids.

"'Is Young Life still going on here?' Ernie asked suddenly.

"'Yes,' I said. 'It's doing well.'

"'That's good,' he said. 'Young people need a place where they can have fun and feel like they belong.'

"'And old people need to remember that little things make a difference.'"

Making a commitment to slow down, smell the flowers along the way, and take advantage of opportunities to change the cultures that are right before our very eyes and then continuing that approach as we move through the other circles of community will be our key to success. By slowing down in this warp-speed culture we begin to give ourselves the chance to look at it through a different lens. Yet our culture currently thrives on speed. And speeding through life is a lot like speeding down a freeway. A lot can be missed.

Have you ever seen the TV show *Mr. Rogers' Neighborhood*? Compare it to *Sesame Street*. Would you agree that there is a little difference? I think more things happen in the first five minutes of *Sesame Street* than happen in the entire *Mr. Rogers* show. I think sometimes it actually takes Mr. Rogers half an hour just to get his shoes off! But Mr. Rogers walks the talk. He focuses upon building relationships. He explains everything. Yes, he seems a geek, but he's a geek that leads with his heart and not with technology. His pace seems oddly out of place in today's environment, but embodied within his style is a nonjudgmental approach, a listening heart, and a genuineness that is refreshing and needed.

One of the messages I get from watching Mr. Rogers is that *being* is just as important as *doing*. Who he is is just as important as what he does. His presence is just as important as what he has to teach. This is just as true with our kids. Not only do they want to know what we know, but they carefully watch to see who we are.

I was having a conversation with a member of the Sioux tribe. He told me that he had a friend who had come over to his house every Saturday for the past three years, and they talked. Chuckling, he said, "You know, to this day, I don't know what he does for a living! It's never been important to us. We enjoy each other's company and have so many other things to talk about." In our culture today, what you "do" is everything. One of the first questions anyone is asked upon meeting someone is "What do you do?" Judgments about the person, decisions about continuing the relationship, in many cases, are decided right there. We live in a culture that, sadly, values "what you do" above everything else. It is an acceptable practice in our culture to work incredibly long hours, take on immense stress, and sacrifice personal and family life. But when I ask kids what the number one thing they want from adults is, the answer is always time. And more time. Our kids need and want adults who know how to start small, go slow, and be with kids. Our kids need adults who know how to do things *with* them, not *to* them.

Our children are mirrors that reflect our culture back to us in myriad ways, and they need all the threads in the tapestry to be strong. I am constantly being asked, "What are some strategies that will help us sustain the vibrancy we want in the circles of community?" Several of these were mentioned in chapter 1, but there are three additional vital strategies we can use that will help sustain these experiences. At first, they don't sound very exciting. But if utilized, they will have a tremendous impact. These strategies are repetition and redundancy. Now, if you had asked me a dozen years ago what I thought about repetition and redundancy, I would have said, "Not interested! I'm into new and improved." But one day I realized the incredible power these two strategies have to transform the environment. Like drops of water constantly dripping upon a stone, they slowly leave their indelible mark.

My revelation came the day I took my kids to see the movie *Flipper*, which, like the television show of the same name, features a dolphin who always saves the day. I was enjoying the film until the camera zoomed in on Flipper cavorting with a Pepsi can in the middle of the beautiful blue Pacific Ocean. As the camera continued to focus on the energetic Flipper and the Pepsi can for several more seconds, I became irritated; but I was inclined to let it go. After all, we see subtle advertisements more and more frequently in movies: cereal boxes in the background, beer cans flashing on the screen, and so on. But a few minutes later, a Pizza Hut delivery man showed up, and I thought, "Wait a minute, aren't those products owned by the same company?" For the rest of the movie I couldn't think about anything else. "I wonder how much Pepsico invested or traded off in order to get its message in front of this target audience," I mused. Then I thought, "Target audience?" I bet Pepsico knew the exact demographics of who would be at the movie. And then I started to worry. I wondered if Pepsico knew I was going to be in that theater with my 2.3 kids because I had been looking for a safe movie to take them to.

Marketers in America understand something that we as parents, neighbors, and community members haven't figured out yet: the power of repetition and redundancy. They understand that in order for their message to be absorbed into the hearts, souls, and minds of our kids, they have to repeat it over and over in a variety of ways. If you missed the Pepsi message in *Flipper,* just switch on the television or drive through your community and see how many businesses have that same message on their signs.

After I had presented the notion of repetition and redundancy to a group in Colorado, a man pulled me aside at a break and said, "Think about NASA for a moment. One thing they really understand at NASA is repetition and redundancy." He went on, "Not only do they have a very high launch-success rate, but NASA's payload is so important that they have numerous, expensive, redundant back-up systems to kick in if one should fail." Then he said, "Aren't our kids our most important payload? Don't they deserve to have positive messages repeated continuously across the community, and shouldn't there be clearly thought-out redundant systems coming from every direction to ensure their safety and support?"

Wouldn't it be exciting if the positive messages a young person was hearing at home were being reinforced at the local school, on the playing field, by businesses, religious institutions, neighbors, and significant adults in that child's life? By consciously and intentionally identifying common values and beliefs we want our children and youth to have and then transmitting them in a variety of creative ways across the community, we give them a great gift.

YouthReach International in Bozeman, Montana started out with a thud. Wanting their kids to experience a life-changing service project, three adults got together, wrote a mission statement, outlined a strategic plan, and were about to announce their intent when they realized something very important was missing—they had forgotten to ask for input from the kids.

Scrapping everything, they restarted the process by inviting teens to come together and talk about service, to decide if it was something they wanted to do, and if so, were they willing to help start a whole new organization where they played key roles. One of the kids' parents who attended an early meeting shook his head over and over and said, "You've got it backward. You need to come up with the plan and then invite the kids. This is no more than a half-baked marshmallow."

Well, three years later, a rotating group of twelve to twenty teens aged fourteen to twenty created their own mission statement, designed their own logo, created a Web site, became involved in numerous local service projects, developed their own code of conduct, and traveled to an orphanage (Ciudad de los Niños) in Hermosillo, Mexico, four times. For almost all of the kids it has been a life-changing experience. One remarked, "It's so unusual to be asked our opinion and for us to be able to help decide almost everything. It's like we're being treated as adults." Another commented, "Our meetings are as much about laughing and having fun as they are about business, and going to Mexico has been the most important event in my life. I mean, these people had so little, but they were willing to give us anything they had." Another teen said, "I cried for hours after leaving. I really fell in love with those kids."

When asked, "What made it so successful?" they all replied, "Adults who were willing to have fun and work at the same time. It always felt like our project and not just theirs!" One adult confided, "Sometimes I didn't want to attend the meetings. But every time, and I mean every time, I came away from the meeting charged by these kids' enthusiasm, energy, and commitment to make the world a better place."

The future of our culture depends upon our getting our priorities straight. Because a healthy culture is directly related to the well-being of its children, we must devote all our energy to creating a culture that values youth. It is so difficult for us to agree on much of anything, but perhaps we can begin our renewal by agreeing upon the truth of the child. Archimedes, known for shouting, "Eureka!" when he recognized a scientific truth, and for his work with levers, said, "Show me a place to stand on and I will move the earth!" We can use this notion by applying it to our own communities. Adults, often unwilling or unable to do something for themselves, will find a way to do things that benefit the children. From personal and informal acts to working with existing structures and organizations, every effort has its impact.

The third strategy I'd recommend is probably the oldest strategy of them all. It's prayer. As a parent there are times when all I can do is turn my kids over to God. And when I read about kids who are destitute, orphaned, and starving, they feel so far away that all I can do is ask for God to hold them in the palm of His hand. It would be a great daily ritual to whisper prayers for our own kids, kids in our communities, and the kids of the world

As we go about consciously and intentionally re-creating our culture, we might want to adopt the eloquent question of the Masai: "And how are the children?" The Masai, considered to be one of the most noble tribes of Africa, have a greeting: "Kasserian Ingera," which means "How are the children?" Whenever members of different tribes meet, the question is asked. This greeting acknowledges the importance the Masai place on their children's well-being. If the answer is "The children are well," it means all is truly well in the tribe. The children are considered a barometer of the health and well-being of all. What if we were to adopt this philosophy and approach? What if we measured the health of our culture and communities based upon the health of our kids? Wouldn't it be wonderful if in the State of the Union address, the president asked before anything else, "How are the children?" and then began to report on their welfare. Or we could start small, and begin with our mayors!

Our kids, in many ways, are our moral conscience. I remember clearly how my brother and I begged our parents to stop smoking. "It's bad for you," we'd implore. We even presented them with figures that showed if they stopped smoking for three years we could buy a boat! I was reminded of this passionate conscience when recently I flipped on the air conditioning in my car, and my daughter went ballistic. "Don't you know, Dad, that by using your air conditioner you are contributing to depletion of the ozone layer?" Humbled, I turned it off.

Children around the world have hopes and dreams of a brave, bold, and sometimes beautiful future. Fifth grader Ethan Sawyer of Atlanta, Georgia, foresees a world where people will only sleep two hours a day.

Maria del Pilar Guzman Sanchez of Mexico, who is ten, predicts a world of "no pollution, no drug addicts, no cocaine addicts, or sexual violence or violence against authorities." Benjamin Mbithi of Kenya, who is eleven, says, "When war comes, I'll just go with my group and make peace. I'll help those people who would have lost their legs or arms by giving those artificial legs. And those people having famine, I will support their areas with food."

And then there is seventeen-year-old Derrick Seaver of Dayton, Ohio, who is too young to vote. Nevertheless, he is running for a seat in the state's legislature. Derrick will turn eighteen by February 6, so he is eligible to compete in the primaries. Totally unfazed, he says, "I know my opponents will talk about what they've done in the past and what I haven't, but I feel this is about the future."

Among all the personal development programs that guarantee life-changing or transformational experiences, none is more transforming than loving our children and learning to be there for them. Nothing can teach patience, unconditional love, compassion, and courage like becoming an advocate for our kids. In his book *Let Us Now Praise Famous Men,* James Agee captured this spirit wonderfully when he said, "In every child who is born, no matter under what circumstances and no matter what parents, the potentiality of the human race is born again."

"Although I am from Venezuela," a bright-eyed mom said, "I have lived in the States for the last twenty years. Until I visited Venezuela this summer I didn't realize how I had accepted attitudes toward children that I didn't really believe. This past summer my young daughter and I traveled there to visit relatives. One afternoon when my daughter and I were walking down a street, we encountered a very beautiful garden. It was quite unusual because most flower gardens in Venezuela are in courtyards so they go unseen. But here was a beautiful flower garden in the front yard of a home!

"A woman, who was on her hands and knees, was busily turning the soil. Feeling our presence, she nodded and smiled at us. As I was admiring her handiwork, suddenly my daughter plucked one of the most radiant flowers in all the garden and said loud enough for both the woman and me to hear: 'Look, Mommy, isn't this special?' Embarrassed, I started to explain to my daughter that these flowers were not for picking and that this woman had worked very hard to grow something so beautiful. As I turned to apologize to the gardener, much to my surprise she was standing right next to me! Registering the panicked look on my face and before I could get a word out, she said very firmly to me, but with great love, 'Don't you know that whenever a child picks a flower, three more grow in its place?'"

NORTH CHICAGO
PUBLIC LIBRARY